PRAISE

"Who'd have thought my delivery of 1 line of dubbing would be the title of a book? — A great read!"

– Brian Drummond: the Ocean Group voice actor of Vegeta

"Reading this book will grant you a deeper understanding of *Dragon Ball Z* and its philosophies. The incredible insights will change the way you view the show forever."

– Alex'sDBZRPG.com

"It's Over 9,000! reinvigorates the franchise. It is a beneficial book for the most jaded of *Dragon Ball Z* fans and non-fans alike."

– iSugoi.com

"For the *Dragon Ball Z* fan, It's Over 9,000! is a must read. Much like how Joseph Campbell related the allegories, myths, and archetypes explored in his masterful *Hero of a Thousand Faces* to George Lucas' *Star Wars* saga, Padula provides an equally fascinating exploration of the themes in *Dragon Ball Z*, imparting insight into just how philosophical and sophisticated the source material truly is."

– Shadowland Magazine

"Hallelujah and praise Kami-sama (or perhaps Shenron) for giving us Derek Padula and his amazingly thorough knowledge of what will always be THE "world-class" anime/manga series."

– MangaTherapy.com

"Embark on a philosophical journey through the world's #1 anime."

– Amazon.com reader review

"Any self-respecting *Dragon Ball* fan must read Derek Padula's books."

– Google Play reader review

"It's a well-written and well-informed exploration that could only come from someone as passionately in love with the shonen epic as many of us are. A stunning service to those looking to turn a scholarly eye to the series, and a great primer for newcomers. From one Vegeta fangirl to the hundreds of others out there, you'll find something to love."

– Japanator.com

This is a *must have* for all DBZ fans! *"When Worldviews Collide"* broadens the already complex world of DBZ by discussing the Buddhist and Daoist elements hidden within the storyline, as well as taking the reader into an in-depth journey through the evolving viewpoints held by both Goku and Vegeta, stemming from their very different upbringings. I was able to re-visit DBZ with more appreciation after reading this book! Don't let the size fool you... this little book packs quite a punch!

– Amazon.com reader review

"Don't think *Dragon Ball Z* has character development? Think again. What's most appealing about this book is the author goes in-depth on the two character's psyche to explain why they are the way they are, why they changed, and what made them so appealing to fans across the world."

– Amazon.com reader review

"If you have *any* questions or inquiries about this fraction of an instant in the *Dragon Ball* Universe, then *this* is the key to unlocking them."

– Apple iBooks reader review

"This author has made me see the universe of *Dragon Ball* and its characters from a perspective that I never imagined, with an in-depth analysis of the different details of this exquisite saga."

– Amazon.es reader review

"Thought you knew *Dragon Ball*? Think again! If you're a fan of *Dragon Ball*, know someone who is, or just want to get to know this ultra popular series better, this is a must read. It's thought-provoking, where the author shows us the deeper side of the *Dragon Ball* Universe. Absolutely love this book, and if your power level is Over 9,000, so will you."

– Google Play reader review

Dragon Ball Z

"It's Over 9,000!"

WHEN WORLDVIEWS COLLIDE

Derek Padula

THEDAOOFDRAGONBALL.COM

Legal Disclaimer

Cataloging In-Publication Data

Padula, Derek.

Dragon Ball Z "It's over 9,000!" when worldviews collide / Derek Padula

Includes bibliographical references and index.

ISBN: 978-0-9831205-3-7

1. Martial arts – Comic books, strips, etc. 2. Heroes. 3. Good and evil. 4. Imaginary wars and battles. 5. Ethics, ancient. 6. Spiritual life – Buddhism. 7. Fantasy comic books, strips, etc. – Japan – 20th century – History and Criticism.

PN6790.J33 – P2 2012

741.5952 – 23

LCCN: 2012916234

Notice of Rights

Notice of Liability

Cover Art Illustrations by Javier Secano.

Book Design by Kat Marriner.

Index by Mary Harper.

Version 1.1

Web: https://thedaoofdragonball.com

Other Books by Derek Padula

Dragon Ball Culture Volume 1: Origin

Dragon Ball Culture Volume 2: Adventure

Dragon Ball Culture Volume 3: Battle

Dragon Ball Culture Volume 4: Westward

Dragon Ball Culture Volume 5: Demons

Dragon Ball Culture Volume 6: Gods

Dragon Ball Culture Volume 7: Anime

Dragon Soul: 30 Years of Dragon Ball Fandom

Dragon Ball Cultura Volumen 1 (Spanish Edition)

Dragon Ball Z "It's Over 9,000!" Cosmovisiones en colisión (Spanish Edition)

All books are available in paperback, hardback, and ebook.

DEDICATION

DEDICATED TO DEBORAH. Thank you for being the Vegeta of my life and pushing me to higher levels.

CONTENTS

FOREWORD

FOR THE ROLE of Vegeta I'm lucky that I didn't have to go through an audition like I normally do. I was asked directly to do his voice and I am very thankful for that.

However, there was this issue where whenever Goku fought with an enemy character, usually that character died after 4 weeks. So I thought 'Okay, I guess this guy is gonna die in a few weeks too,' but I figured it would be better to give this character my best shot, to breathe life into Vegeta and make him the ultimate villain.

In Japanese there are many different ways of saying "I" and "You" (similar to saying thou, thee, or ye in English, but Japanese has way more and each of them are used in different situations), and I was careful not to use vulgar words that would make the character sound like some average villain. I intentionally used words that would sound more sophisticated yet intimidating, as a consummate villain should.

As for "Over 9,000!", to be honest, as a Japanese I'm not so sure what it is about that line that people like so much and why it became so popular, hahaha. In fact, I would have loved for someone to explain it to me like Derek does in this book.

But still, even though it was not my intention for that line to get so popular, me being the voice of that character, it makes me very happy that people enjoyed it so much.

I feel very honored and lucky that I had the chance to play Vegeta, a character that is loved by so many people around the world.

I am very grateful for that.

Ryo Horikawa
堀川りょう
2012

INTRODUCTION

THE *DRAGON BALL Z* internet phenomenon known as "It's Over 9,000!" went viral with over 7 million views on YouTube in the late 2000's. *Dragon Ball Z "It's Over 9,000!" When Worldviews Collide* will explain the meaning behind "It's Over 9,000!", its significant pop cultural implications in mass media, and provide deep insights into what made the scene it's based on so important.

If you have heard the term "It's Over 9,000!" on the Internet or from somebody saying it in person, you may have laughed, been a bit confused, or started saying it yourself! In any case I can tell you with confidence that you're still missing a lot of the story. In this book you'll learn exactly *why* "It's Over 9,000!" became so popular and you'll discover what happens between two Saiya-jins when worldviews collide.

PART 1 "IT'S OVER 9,000!"

In Part 1 you will learn what "It's Over 9,000!" is, where it originated, and how it became so popular in the modern pop cultural landscape.

PART 2 WHEN WORLDVIEWS COLLIDE: GOKU VERSUS VEGETA

Underlying themes prevalent in the *Dragon Ball Z* series make their debut in a meme. It is through scenes of conflict in characters that these themes come to life and engage the viewer. Two of the most prominent characters in the series, Goku and Vegeta, will be examined to show how their epic rivalry is a catalyst for profound growth.

PART 3 A THIN SLICE OF *DRAGON BALL*

If "It's Over 9,000!" represents a single letter of this evolving pop cultural language, than the *Dragon Ball* series embodies this unique alphabet. The significance lies in the community this creates, a language that is now understood by millions of fans that contribute to the identity of the collective and the individual.

The "It's Over 9,000!" phenomenon is thus a microcosm of the epic *Dragon Ball* phenomenon. This book is just one of an even richer collection of stories that are further revealed in *The Dao of Dragon Ball* book.

The journey of "Over 9,000" miles starts with a single turn of the page.

PART I

"OVER 9,000!"

DRAGON BALL Z is an extremely influential Japanese anime and pop culture success. The action packed television series reached its peak in Japan from 1990 to 1996 and in the United States from 1999 to 2003. This book gives an inside look into how one viewer transformed a typical Dragon Ball Z episode into a shorter clip that exploded in popularity on *YouTube*, receiving over 7 million views. The content of this video inspired a common pop culture Internet joke, or meme, called "It's over 9,000!" that spread around the world.

In episode 21 of *Dragon Ball Z*, Vegeta and Nappa, the two Saiya-jin aliens, have invaded Earth seeking the dragon balls so that they can have their wish for immortality granted by Shenron (Chinese: *Shénlóng*, 神龍), the God Dragon. Goku, the hero of the series, stands in their way, and they want to determine Goku's battle power before they fight.

Vegeta uses his "Scouter" (Japanese: *Sukautā*, スカウター), an advanced energy-detecting device that tracks the number of an opponent's battle power level. Vegeta watches Goku's number increase rapidly as it rises up to power level 8,000 and then to over 9,000. Vegeta screams, "It's over 9,000!" and breaks his Scouter in rage.

Over nine years after its premiere in the United States, a humorously edited video of this segment was placed on *YouTube* and went viral. Through social media, "It's over 9,000!" became a popular meme and is now a global Internet term that people use to describe anything of high quantity.

This book explains the "It's over 9,000!" phenomenon.

THE ORIGINAL "IT'S OVER 9,000!"

To better understand the "It's over 9,000!" phenomenon, we have to review the source material that was used to create it. Namely, the episode that the clip was taken from.

In the original *Dragon Ball Z* episode, the Saiya-jins, Nappa and Vegeta, threaten Earth's people and have already caused great damage. Up to this point in time Goku has been training in the afterlife with the celestial being, North Kaiō. After hastily returning to Earth, Goku speeds toward the battleground hoping that he can make it in time.

When Goku arrives, he sees that many of his allies and lifelong friends have already died in the battle, and he is extremely upset at the news. He "powers up" with anger and prepares for the fight.

The environment around Goku begins to react to his incredible energy. Vegeta's Scouter picks up on Goku's rising energy and begins making noises while flashing numbers on the panel in front of his eyes.

The original scene of the American English dub occurs in episode 21 of the first season of *DBZ*, first aired on April 26, 1997. Here is the dialogue:

> **Goku:** "GREAAAAAAARRRGGHHH!" *Powers up.*
>
> **Vegeta:** "Power level's ... 8,000. Huh? Now, it's over nine."
>
> **Goku:** "YEAAAAAAGHHH!" *Finishes powering up. The rocks levitating in the air fall down and the dust clears.*
>
> **Nappa:** "Vegeta, what does the Scouter say about his power level?"
>
> **Vegeta:** *Takes the Scouter off his head.* "It's over 9,000!" *Crushes the Scouter in his hand.*
>
> **Nappa:** "What, 9,000?! There's no way that can be right, can it?!"

That's the entire scene. It was just one of many in the 508 episodes of the *Dragon Ball* series and warranted no special attention or recognition.

However, nine years later, an edited version was created by a *YouTube* user, Kajetokun, and posted on October 17, 2006, called "9000!! NINE THOUSAAAAANDD!" This innocuous 30-second clip was looped continuously, chopped up, slowed down, sped up, and made into a highly comedic two-and-a-half-minute-long video.[1] The original post on *You-Tube* received over 5 million views as of June 28, 2009, and continued to spread globally. As of June 29, 2012, the original "It's over 9,000!" video by Kajetokun had over 7.1 million views.

During the rise of the meme's popularity, the *Japanator.com* website interviewed Kajetokun on April 30, 2008. Kajetokun said, "I had no idea it was going to get this big. Really, it was just a small little something I made as an inside joke for my friends. My friend Patrick posted it on [*4Chan. org's*] /*b*/, and then I ended up having, like, 20,000 views the next day. Then Scott from *VGcats.com* front page linked [to] my video, and I woke up to 200,000 views." It started to rise considerably from that point on.

As a result of its popularity, a previously nonexistent term became a searchable phrase. According to *Google Trends*, search queries in the last quarter of 2008 for the shortened term "over 9000" rose steeply, especially during the week of September 22.

The video was subsequently remixed, spoofed, and transformed by others, and it took on a life of its own. Live-action scenes were filmed, 3D models were rendered, and random combinations of different versions from various sources have been thrown together all over the Web.

For those unfamiliar with the series, the scene may not make any sense when taken out of context. However, the meme connected with non–*Dragon Ball Z* viewers in the humorous way that it was replicated, which was a significant reason why it caught on like wildfire.

This creative act of sharing through social media resulted in something quite interesting. The video reached a new demographic of Internet-savvy users previously unfamiliar with Japanese anime, introducing *Dragon Ball Z* to millions more.

---

1   See the Resources page at the end of this book for links to the videos.

THE ORIGINAL "OVER 9,000!" WAS REALLY "OVER 8,000!"

For most casual viewers unfamiliar with the Japanese version, they would have no idea that the term "Over 9,000!" was wrong to begin with. But it was! In the original Japanese anime, manga, and newly "refreshed" version of *Dragon Ball Z* (known as *Dragon Ball Kai*) Goku's power level was specifically stated as being "Over 8,000!"

In episode 28 of the Japanese *DBZ* anime (aired November 29, 1989) and episode 12 of the *Kai* anime series (aired June 21, 2009), the scene proceeds as follows:

> **Goku:** "YEAAAAAARRRRGGHHHH!" *Powers up.*

> **Vegeta:** "Battle power is 7,000 ... 8,000 ... Impossible!"

> **Goku:** "YEARGHHH!" *Finishes powering up. The rocks levitating in the air fall down and the dust clears.*

> **Nappa:** "Vegeta! What's the reading on Kakarotto's battle power now?"[2]

> **Vegeta:** *Takes the Scouter off his head.* "It's over 8,000!" *Crushes the Scouter in his hand.*

> **Nappa:** "Over 8,000?! There must be some mistake! It must be broken!"

Why the difference in translation for the English anime?

The common answer available on the Internet is that the anime was dubbed in English as "9,000" because the sound of "nine" worked better with Vegeta's mouth movements than "eight." This seems plausible because dubbing companies frequently replace lines with ones they feel are more appropriate or synchronize better with the animation.

---

2   Kakarotto (Kakarot in the FUNimation dub) is Goku's original Saiya-jin name before being adopted and raised on earth. Vegeta and Nappa only refer to Goku with his Saiya-jin name.

However, if you look at the actual animation, this isn't so plausible. The mouth movements are simple and both "eight" and "nine" could have been vocalized by the shape of Vegeta's mouth. So it is unclear why the change was made, and it could have possibly just been a mistake.

What is interesting is that years later, in 2004, during a redubbing of *Dragon Ball Z*'s early episodes, the supposed mistake was replicated. FUNimation had years of experience with the series at this point and should have been fully aware of the original Japanese phrase, voiced by Ryō Horikawa. Nevertheless, their *Ultimate Uncut Edition* DVDs repeated the "It's over 9,000!" line with their own cast, with Vegeta played by Christopher Sabat. But fans were not as happy with this rendition as they were with the video clip used by Kajetokun in the original video, where Vegeta was played by Brian Drummond of the Ocean Group voice acting company from Canada. The reason most often given by fans for this preference is that they prefer Drummond's over-the-top extension of "nine thousaa-aaandd." Similarly edited "It's over 9,000!" clips using the FUNimation actors were not as popular.

As time passed and the fandom for "It's over 9,000!" grew, FUNimation became very familiar with the meme. They capitalized on it to promote their *Dragon Box* releases of the *Dragon Ball Z* series in 2009. The promotional trailer was narrated by Christopher Sabat as Vegeta, who said, "Can you feel the *Dragon Box*'s power? It's over 9,000!"

Because *Dragon Ball* kept being rereleased in different formats, in 2010, FUNimation redubbed the scene in English once again for the "refreshed" *Dragon Ball Z Kai*. But this time they dubbed two versions. In the televised version, Vegeta said "It's over 9,000!" while on the uncut DVDs he said "It's over 8,000!" FUNimation was well aware of the meme's popularity in society and wanted the public to be happy, so they redubbed it incorrectly on purpose because it was so popularly accepted to be "It's over 9,000!" rather than "It's over 8,000!" The DVD buyers were a smaller and more hard-core audience that FUNimation believed would prefer the proper "It's over 8,000!" Yet this caused a problem, as some of the fans actually wanted it to be "It's over 9,000!" because of their adoration for the meme.

This means that FUNimation, one of the largest anime and voice-over companies in the world, changed the way they did business in order to ride the wave of the "It's over 9,000!" meme's success. They were influenced by a *Dragon Ball* Internet meme created by a single person's video that went viral.

The fact that FUNimation successfully dubbed the line as "It's over 8,000!" shatters the argument that it was impossible for Vegeta to say "8,000" because of the mouth movements. They could have done it before in the original dub, but if they had, then we wouldn't have the term "It's over 9,000!" today!

"OVER 9,000!" OF WHAT?

What does "It's over 9,000!" even mean? Nine thousand of what?

If you watch the video or read the manga, you'll see a unique-looking device attached to the side of Vegeta's head, called the Scouter. The Saiya-jin use the Scouter to detect and quantify a living being's combined physical, emotional, and spiritual energy at a given time.

Scouters are used immediately after landing on a planet to scout the locations of possible threats or targets of attack, such as powerful warriors or cities filled with people. How and what type of energy frequency it analyzes is unspecified, as is the unit of measurement. Supposedly it detects a life frequency, known in Japanese as *ki*, and translates this into a number, which the *Dragon Ball* warriors in the original Japanese refer to as *sentō-ryoku* (戦闘力). The term can be translated into English as "combat power," "fighting strength," "battle power" or "power level."

This *ki* (気, pronounced "kee") is a Japanese term for a universal life force believed to be found in all beings, and one that can be developed and strengthened through training. In East Asian martial arts and medical theories, *ki* is found in every cell of the untold billions within the body, as well as in the combined life experience and spiritual energy of the being. The greater the life force (*ki*), the greater the power level.

Ki is paradoxically both an ephemeral, invisible energy, as well as a material, visible substance. Not all people can feel or see it. Through training in special exercise and meditation regimens, it is generally believed that a person can become increasingly sensitive to *ki*. It has electric, warm, magnetic qualities, described as heat, wind, or perceived as light, and it can push, pull, or flow like water. It is also related to a person's inner spirit and mood. In this sense, *ki* is a material substance, a life force, and an energy form all in one.

All beings in *Dragon Ball* have *ki* and it is simply a matter of training hard to develop it. After a certain point of training, this energy can be projected out of the body as a material weapon or in various other ways, such as self powered flight.

For reference, in *Dragon Ball,* the overweight yet physically active farmer at the beginning of *Dragon Ball Z* had a power level of 5 before being killed by Goku's brother, Raditz, who had a power level of approximately 1,200.

WHY IS POWER LEVEL IMPORTANT?

Aside from using it when sizing up their opponents, Saiya-jins use power level to determine the relative strength of their own children at birth so as to classify them within their caste-based social order. Since they are a warrior race, this is how they determine who is valuable and who is not.

Vegeta and Nappa were both born into royal families. Vegeta informs Goku that he was born into a low caste and sent off to another planet because of his low power level. Vegeta is the royal prince and strongest of his race, and Nappa is the general of the entire Saiya-jin army. The fact that Goku, a low-caste Saiya-jin, now has a power level over 8,000 is a slap in the face to Vegeta and Nappa.

Nappa has a power level of 4,000 and Vegeta has a power level of 18,000. This is why Nappa freaks out while Goku remains confident. It's why Vegeta is so upset and screams "It's over 8,000!" and then smashes his Scouter. Vegeta isn't afraid, he's just especially surprised and annoyed by Goku's rapid growth, because less than a year earlier, Goku had a power level of only 334 while fighting against Raditz. And how could a low-class Saiya-jin have such power? Goku's incredible change was a result of his training in the afterlife with North Kaiō, master of the northern quadrant of the universe.

In *Dragon Ball Kai*, Nappa gets beaten down and punched into a small mountain by Goku. He yells, "Damn you to Hell!" to which Goku calmly responds, "I see now. As expected, you're not that tough." Nappa shouts back, "I'm an elite warrior from a noble family! I won't allow some low-class trash like you to make fun of nobility like me! You're gonna' pay! I'll freakin' kill you!" Nappa's self image and pride are threatened by Goku's existence, and in order to validate himself, Nappa has to kill this "low-class trash." In *Dragon Ball Z*, a warrior's pride becomes a matter of life and death.

Another reason why Vegeta and Nappa are so surprised by the Scouter's readout is that Scouters do not measure suppressed or potential energy, only the amount of energy that is emanating from a living being at the time of detection. Most fighters in *Dragon Ball* do not know how to hide their true power or draw forth what's lying dormant inside. Through intense training with Kami (Japanese: 神), the spiritual God of earth, and Mister Popo (his assistant), Goku and the other earthlings learned how to suppress or draw forth their power during a battle. This gives them an advantage over warriors who rely on external technology, such as the Scouter, which may provide misleading readings or fail to detect a warrior that has hidden their *ki*.

Thus, as the series progresses, the power levels read by Scouters start to become unreliable. In addition, if a being's power level increases too sharply, the Scouter experiences an electrical overload and explodes. Another benefit of their spiritual training is that Goku and other characters such as Krillin and Tenshinhan are able to internally sense and gauge a being's *ki* without a Scouter anyway. Eventually the external Scouters are rendered obsolete, as new characters are introduced with internal energy tracking devices or abilities.

So now that you understand why power levels are so important to the series and to this scene in particular, let's take another look at the meme in the real world.

"IT'S OVER 9,000!" IN THE REAL WORLD

The sudden popularity of the "It's Over 9,000!" video started a new trend on the Internet: using the expression to refer to anything of a large number or great quantity.

The pattern of speaking this way always began with a question containing a reference to the Scouter and an unknown value. Nappa's line was the basis of the question, and Vegeta's line was the answer. For example: "What does the Scouter say about his ___?" The reply would be, "It's over 9,000!"

As time went on, the joke gradually evolved from the formulaic call and response to a more general question and answer. And the "It's" was dropped. For instance, "How many people were at the concert last night?" The other person responds, "Over 9,000!" implying that there were a *lot* of people at the concert.

Soon there were other ways to use this phrase, such as, "The number of views on this video just reached over 9,000!" and "My bank account just reached over 9,000!"

"Over 9,000!" started to appear on mashups of other memes, like LOL Cats, and eventually on clothing such as shirts and hats.

On the opposite side of the spectrum, there is also the less common derivative "Under 9,000!" For example, "What does the Scouter say about the Dow Jones stock index? It's under 9,000!"

The fame of this video and vernacular grew on the Internet and slowly started to trickle into mainstream culture. It was even alluded to by Michael Jordan in a commercial spot for Nike, when he said, "I've missed more than 9,000 shots in my career. ... And that is why I succeed."

This term entered the casual American landscape in a tangential and more offensive way when it appeared on *Oprah* on September 19, 2008. Oprah's latest target of the week was child pornographers and pedophiles. Oprah was discussing the effect they had on our society, and she said, "Let me read you something that was posted on our message board from someone who claims to be a member of a known pedophile network. It said this, 'He doesn't forgive, he does not forget, his group has over 9,000 penises ... and they are all raping children.'"

In truth, the message was posted by "Anonymous," the archetypal username of members of the *4Chan* website, the birthplace of many Internet memes and infamous trollers and hackers of pop culture icons. This was the same website where Kajetokun's "It's over 9,000!" video premiered. The message was planted on Oprah's message board and Oprah took the bait, finding it and reading it on national TV. This moment is a classic example of what's known as "Internet trolling," and one that was subsequently exploited across the Net with many follow-up jokes. The event itself is now called "Oprah 9,000!"

It was around this time that "Over 9,000!" reached its zenith of popularity.

The pop culture anime *Dragon Ball Z* inspired a remix by Kajetokun on *YouTube*, which was then reassimilated by the spinoff video game *Dragon Ball Z: Burst Limit* in 2008, in which Bandai Namco re-created the scene of Goku's fight with the Saiya-jins in full 3D. The English voice actors at FUNimation redubbed the scene once again with the incorrect "Over 9,000!"—most likely because they chose to give fans what they had come to love.

Dragon Ball Z has also been the source material for several other parodies and video remixes, such as "The Balls are Inert," and "I'ma Firin' Mah Lazah," otherwise known as "Shoop da Whoop." However, none have been as popular as "It's over 9,000!"

Internet trends change quickly, and despite its sudden rise in popularity, by mid-2009 the meme and all catchphrases derived from it were considered passé or cliché, and were only popular in certain locations of Japanese interest on the Web, such as anime, manga, and video game sites or products.

For example, it was used in the Sony PSP game *Prinny: Can I Really Be the Hero?* In this game, the descriptive text for the character CHEFBOT-9000 says, "Guess what the scouter says about his power level. It's OVER NINE TH—okay, sorry, I just can't do it."

As a more current example, in November 2011, independent reporter Tim Pool broadcast a live feed of the Occupy Wall Street movement in New York City on *Ustream*, an online streaming service. The number of viewers kept rising, higher and higher, and when the number of viewers passed 9,000, the reporter said, "We've gone over 9,000!" Suddenly, the viewers started to leave dozens of comments in the message board, referencing the "Over 9,000!" joke.

Also in November 2011, Freddie Wong, a filmmaker and *YouTube* superstar, posted a live-action version of the "Over 9,000!" video on the Internet as a reward to those who pledged money to his *Video Game High School* Web series. It stars himself and a friend dressed as the Saiya-jins in full costumes and with special effects. As of August 8, 2012 the video has had over 7.5 million views, which is more than the original video it was based on.

And yet despite its relative drop in popularity, the phrase "Over 9,000!" is still widely spoken in pop culture and urban slang. Several video mashups with other memes have been developed and the term is now common vernacular of the Millennial Generation. Look on Urban Dictionary or do a simple search on Twitter and you will see its many variations in casual conversation.

THE PERFECT CATCHPHRASE

Because the scene was dubbed incorrectly and then turned into a joke, "Over 9,000!" resulted in a perfect example of how a popular anime catchphrase can stand alone as an Internet phenomenon.

Yet there's more to the "Over 9,000!" story than meets the eye. In Part 2 of this book you'll discover how the scene between Goku and Vegeta was the result of their different worldviews colliding, the prelude to an epic rivalry, and the fundamental source of their growth.

WHEN WORLDVIEWS COLLIDE: GOKU VERSUS VEGETA

THE "IT'S OVER 9,000!" video seems simple and humorous, but there's much more going on behind the scenes than the viewer may be aware of. Part of the popularity of "It's over 9,000!" stems from an underlying theme present throughout *Dragon Ball*—the power of an individual's untapped potential—which manifests in clashing worldviews, conflict and polar character development.

Considering that both Goku and Vegeta are full blooded Saiya-jins, why do they oppose one another? In order to fully understand why the scene depicted in "It's over 9,000!" is so important, we need to delve into the two worldviews and the warriors they produced.

In Part 2 you will learn how "It's over 9,000!" shows the dichotomy between worldviews colliding and points to several underlying themes inherent in *Dragon Ball Z* and our own humanity.

You will see that it's not as simple as "good guy" fights "bad guy." You're about to discover exactly why Goku and Vegeta were destined for conflict and why the scene depicted in "It's over 9,000!" is such an important part of the *Dragon Ball* story.

2.1 GROWTH THROUGH CONFLICT

There is no growth without conflict. And there is no greater conflict in storytelling than an ideological, class-based, external vs. internal, hard vs. soft, fist-to-fist brawl! It is through conflict that Goku and Vegeta are able to increase their power level and refine their character.

The primary cause of conflict in *Dragon Ball* comes from differences in ideological mindsets, whether it's the difference between the Turtle School and Crane School ethics or Piccolo Daimaŏ's desire to conquer the Earth and Goku's decision to stop him. These worldviews collide and cause violent, combative conflicts.

The original *Dragon Ball* is a mix of fantastical Kung Fu legends with Japanese and American pop culture. *Dragon Ball Z* introduces aliens into the fold, complicating things further. At this point it shifts from different factions on Earth fighting against one another, to all of Earth united against an alien threat. There are now two worldviews in conflict–earthlings who believe in a person's inner potential, and aliens who judge a person at birth.

On Earth, everyone is born more or less equal and has the potential to rise up and shape their own lives. A person is not limited by their genetics. Earthlings judge others by their actions, and the spiritual warriors on Earth intuitively feel the power of others expressed at any given moment, whether it's positive or negative. They look upon others holistically and understand that everyone has ups and downs, like a wave, so it is important to see past current behaviors and believe in their potential.

In contrast, the aliens believe that people are fixed at birth and will amount to nothing more than what they start with. There is no amount of hard work that can overcome their classification. The Saiya-jins have an altogether different worldview from the earthlings because theirs is a paradigm built on social structure maintained through power: Where strength is all that matters. The Saiya-jin society was assimilated by Lord Freeza when he subjugated their civilization. He placed their already power based social framework into an even larger power based social hierarchy, with himself at the top. Suddenly the Saiya-jins not only had to compete with themselves for the position of top monkey, but also the other aliens and mutants within the Empire. It's a place where life and death are determined by power level alone, measured and judged by an external scientific device called the Scouter.

The universal life energy called *ki* bonds these two worldviews together. Daoism and East Asian martial arts state that *ki* is found in all forms of matter throughout the universe and can be cultivated by anyone. Both cultures use their own form of mind-body science to develop and refine *ki*. *Ki* is a subtle language that everyone understands, yet they understand it in different ways owing to their different self-cultivation systems.

In the case of Goku and Vegeta, not only are they both *ki* cultivation practitioners, they're also full blooded Saiya-jins. They love to fight, push themselves in extreme challenges and almost die in the process, only to rise up stronger. Deep in their Saiya-jin sub-conscious there is no greater joy or purpose in life. Nevertheless, they are completely different in how they view themselves and others.

The significance of the "It's over 9,000!" scene lies in how it exposes these worldviews through conflict.

Let's start by turning our eye toward Vegeta, the Prince of all Saiya-jins.

2.2 VEGETA'S PERSPECTIVE - THROUGH THE LENS OF A SCOUTER

Vegeta's worldview is the result of being raised in a power struggle society built atop the fusion of external scientific technology and mind-body science.

This book isn't about summarizing the entire history of Saiya-jin society or of Vegeta's life. For that you can go to the Internet or the series itself. Instead, here's the short version of the parts that formed Vegeta's worldview.

The Saiya-jins (the vegetable people) originally lived on Planet Plant with the Tsufuru-jins (the fruit people).[1] The Saiya-jins were strong but barbaric and the Tsufuru-jins were physically weak yet highly scientific. There was a 10 year war and the vegetables proved stronger than the fruits. The Tsufuru-jins were annihilated and the Saiya-jins renamed it Planet Vegeta, in honor of King Vegeta, father of Prince Vegeta.

Afterward, their undeveloped society was assimilated into the Freeza Empire under the promise that they would be taken care of and allowed to battle new opponents all over the galaxy, forever enjoying their lives as warriors.[2] The remaining technology of the Tsufuru-jins was assimilated into the Freeza Empire, including the Scouters they used in battle.

The Scouter would ironically become synonymous with the Saiya-jins themselves, even though their original nature (before meeting Freeza) was to abhor technology and rely exclusively on their own internal strength. They are introduced in the series wearing Scouters, so the audience associates them with the device, but it does not originate from their own culture.

Why is that important to "It's over 9,000!"? Because what the Saiya-jins actually received was subjugation under a despotic overlord: A being who told them what to do, what planet to conquer and who to fight. Freeza was so concerned that the Saiya-jin's incredible fighting potential may get out of control that he analyzed their powers at birth in order to main-

---

1   The Japanese term Tsufuru-jin (ツフル人) is a name pun by Toriyama, referencing the English word of fruit, transliterated as *furutsu* and rearranged. The name humorously contrasts the Saiya-jin (サイヤ人), another rearranged name pun referencing the Japanese word for vegetable, *yasai*. The FUNimation dub refers to their race as Tuffles, which is a play on the fungi called truffles. It is not common knowledge that truffles are the "fruit body" of the fungi, so this unfortunately dilutes the humorous dichotomy between the two opposing races on Planet Plant that Toriyama intended.

2   There is no official name for the Freeza Empire in the original Japanese, so "Freeza Empire" is a term born out of necessity. Nevertheless, foreign fans have unofficially (and debatably) referred to it as the "Planet Trade Organization" or "World Trade Organization," as it is in the business of cleansing and selling planets. Surprisingly such a business transaction is never shown in the series, only referred to by Raditz and others as their raison d'etre.

tain his dominance. All the while this despot profited at their expense and offered no alternative other than death.

Freeza created a society where scientists measure a person's power level with an external device to determine their internal worth. Every Saiya-jin is subjected to this test. The ones with a passing grade are allowed to stay and placed into an appropriate class. Vegeta for example had a high power level at birth and is a self-declared "super elite." Those at the other end of the spectrum are considered social trash and sent to outlying planets with the intent that they would grow up, become strong, and kill everyone, making the planet easier for Freeza's men to conquer and sell. This is Goku; a disposable piece of garbage sent to cleanse Earth.

In a class based society like Freeza's, people don't have the opportunity to live up to their potential. No other characteristic of a person's mind is important in this society. Will they be talented artists? Are they compassionate listeners or soulful singers? It doesn't matter. All that matters is ones power level at birth measured by the Scouter. This isn't to say Freeza's society doesn't have scientists or intelligent thinkers, because we see that there are medics, pilots and other engineers, but in a military based society filled with warriors, the intelligentsia are merely the oil used to keep the war machine running.

Freeza viewed the Saiya-jins as menial servants, and the Saiya-jins were kept blissfully ignorant of their situation. Under false pretense they did Freeza's grunt work for little more than their own survival, and yet many of them believed in the illusion and were grateful for it. Their basic needs were being met and their Saiya-jin desire to fight and kill was being satiated. Seemed like a good deal.

Truthfully, the Saiya-jins experienced segregation based on a number that in practice is no different than segregation by skin color or any other external factor. Freeza disliked the Saiya-jins for being savages and he feared their power in numbers, but he gladly took advantage of their desire to fight. He skillfully maintained the illusion that they were better off than before by rewarding them with feelings of accomplishment, such as a higher rank in the army with more responsibility. Freeza harnessed their primal strength through this external form of psychological manipulation.

The illusion was that they could somehow improve their lives within Freeza's hierarchy, but it was a lie from the beginning because they were judged through the lens of a Scouter and classified at birth. A man's entire identity was fixed, static and unchanging.

It was slavery. Freeza was a foreigner who annexed the natives from their home, gave them technology and put them to work for nothing more than food, shelter, and a false sense of purpose.

Whether intentional by Akira Toriyama or not, it's easy to see the correlations between this story and our own world history. Freeza, a white alien, profited off the sweat and blood of what he often described as "monkeys," by promising a better future in a new frontier.

The class structure concept was a fabricated paradigm used to enforce his will on others and maintain power. It's a social and behavioral framework that is all too relatable, and it's one that all Saiya-jins went along with. The groupthink mentality towed the line of the status quo or the complicit will of King Vegeta. And according to Freeza, "high class" or not, they were still just "filthy monkeys."

By the time King Vegeta enlightened to his reality and decided to rebel against his "master," it was too late. The beginning of the Saiya-jin persecution and the end for the Saiya-jin race had already begun.

2.2.1 FATHER FIGURES

Freeza killed Vegeta's father when he was 5 years old, along with the destruction of his home planet and the genocide of his entire race. According to the canon storyline by Toriyama, the only 4 survivors were Vegeta, Nappa, Raditz and Goku, because they were each on a planet cleansing mission at the time of the mass killing.

Freeza kept Vegeta around because he was especially cold hearted, obedient and useful. As a child, when Nappa first contacts Vegeta through Scouter (also a communication device) to announce the destruction of Planet Vegeta by "collision with a meteor" (repeating the lie he had been told by Freeza's men), Vegeta's response is telling of his character. He says, "... and?" as if there was supposed to be some reason why he should care. Even Nappa, a murderer of countless innocent people, is surprised that Vegeta shows no concern. He didn't care that his father and all his people died. Instead he learned a cold, hard lesson about the thin line between life and death. Power is everything.

Under Freeza's wing he was sent on one mission after the next, continuously fighting and learning to rely on his own strength and power while crushing those who are judged to be inferior. He would land on a planet, scan everyone with the Scouter, and then kill them. He dutifully obeyed Freeza's orders, yet in Freeza's eyes he was still just a Saiya-jin and therefore nothing more than a tool. Vegeta went without a strong father figure his entire life. Instead he was raised by a power hungry and strict despot from another race.

It could be argued that King Vegeta was perhaps not altogether different from Freeza, and that given the opportunity to rule such a large empire he would have treated Vegeta the same way. However, while we do know that he was ruthless to his subordinates and delighted in the death of others, he was also proud of his son and wanted him to grow up strong. In episode 124 of *Dragon Ball Z* called "I Will Overcome Goku!! The King of the Saiya-jin Warrior Race," there is a flashback scene where King Vegeta and a 5 year old Vegeta are watching the Saiya-jins blast off into space on their way toward conquering other planets. He says to his son, "You, Prince, your abilities were the highest of anyone's, that of a super elite Saiya-jin!" The King's face fills with pride and he says, "You are certain to become the greatest Saiya-jin in the universe! In fact, you may even become the Legendary Super Saiya-jin!" This elitist mentality was instilled into Vegeta by his father. He taught Vegeta that he was not only born talented, he was better than everyone else and would one day become the most powerful being in existence. It was only a matter of time.

As Vegeta grows up under Freeza's heel, he starts to learn the truth and it changes his personality. He matures and poignantly realizes that he is the sole survivor of the Saiya-jin royal family and his entire race is gone and never coming back. For all he knows it's just him, Nappa, and the low class warrior Raditz that remain of his once proud race. His position in life as a royal "super elite" becomes interwoven with his self-identity. Vegeta believes he comes from a privileged background and was born with inherent abilities and intelligence superior to others. This belief is validated with each opponent or victim he kills on the battlefield. He becomes bitter, hate filled and antagonistic against anyone who disrespects the pride he feels for himself and his now deceased Saiya-jin people. Vegeta doesn't serve other men, other men serve Vegeta, the Prince of all Saiya-jins!

Unfortunately Vegeta happens to be serving Freeza, so while under his master he secretly plots to kill him. He hated Freeza for reasons other than the death of his people. Vegeta wanted to kill Freeza because his *pride* wouldn't allow someone to be stronger than himself. He grew to hate Freeza above all others because he was the boss man at the top. Too weak to enact revenge yet unable to escape the system, Vegeta bided his time until the right moment to strike.

As an extremely strong willed individual filled with Saiya-jin pride, Vegeta eventually rebels against Freeza and his subordinates, just as his father had done before. Although he is a "super elite" in Freeza's dominion and was treated better than his military cohorts, he still strives to overthrow Freeza. Vegeta is filled with hatred and pride and these push him to take action and change his situation.

This is the origin of Vegeta, an angry man determined to rule supreme in the universe.

2.2.2 HUMAN NATURE IN ACTION

It is human nature to categorize. Seemingly embedded in our genetic code is the intrinsic need to quantify and measure our reality to then find our place in it and navigate around. It helps us make sense of the world. This is exactly why the Saiya-jins and other aliens within Freeza's empire use the Scouter to navigate new worlds and encounters.

The psychologist William James states in *The Varieties of Religious Experience: A Study in Human Nature* (1902), "The first thing an intellect does with an object is to classify it along with something else." As children we learn to categorize the objects around us. An apple is a fruit, a flower is a plant, a dog is an animal. Likewise as adults we first categorize people and places, and only then do we know how to interact. For example, the social responses we give to an animal are far different than to a gentleman. Observing differences among people and categorizing them (or choosing not to) is what leads to the development of a unique worldview.

Try to imagine living in a society like Vegeta's where power is all that matters and self worth is defined by a number. All the warriors identify or interact with others with their own number and the number of the other person in mind. The first thing they do when they meet someone new is measure them with the Scouter. Likewise, the first thing they do after landing on a new planet is check the Scouter for high power levels. It is a habitual, reflexive action.

The Saiya-jins, mutants and other aliens in Freeza's empire use Scouters as a tool for external categorizing and validation among their peers. The number tells them, "This person is below me, and that's how they should be treated." By stating the number out loud they validate their own existence and push down others with a lower number. How can the number be denied? It can be pointed to in the device as proof. Thus, the external pressure of rivalries is unwillingly forced upon them by the knowledge that they are superior to a person below and inferior to a person above, whomever that may be. It's then socially implied that there should be a desire to suppress the person below and topple the person above. This is a recipe for instant class struggle.

In the alien worldview, people are applied a fixed number and then classified accordingly. Freeza is on top and everyone else is below. The closer to the top you are, the better your life will be. Personal power and higher social position can still be gained through fighting and training, but you will be judged at every step of the way, and if you step too far out of line then you will be disciplined or killed.

This worldview breeds ruthless judgment, selfish opportunism, split second reactive violence, and compassionless decisions where they would gladly stab a former ally in the back in order to rise higher up the ladder. It also creates a society drowning in absolutes and explains why they are always so surprised when someone has a power level greater than their previous perception of the person. They speak with firm denials, saying "Impossible!" "It can't be!" and "The Scouter must be broken!"

What does this tell us about the nature of this alien society? In a world where everyone has a Scouter in front of their eyes, everyone else will look like a number! That simple number allows them to quickly categorize others and treat them accordingly. What is a person if not that number? They're a complicated mix of contradictions, truths and lies, strengths and weaknesses, loves and hates, and an endless supply of emotions. They're people!

Even Goku's father cared nothing for his son. In *Dragon Ball Z: Bardock, The Father of Goku* TV Special (1990), his squad mates ask Bardock if he would like to go back to Planet Vegeta and visit his newborn child. Bardock says "To see the lowest-class warrior without any promise at all? What kind of fool would make that trip?" This is what the Scouter does, it strips people of their worth and turns them into a number. A society built upon these numbers denies its own humanity. How fitting that in *Dragon Ball* this society consists of aliens and mutants. There is no "human" among them.

It also tells us that if we only pay attention to that which is measurable through external instruments, then we'll become blind to the wonders of potential and possibility in all that isn't. In life, what you see matters much less than how you see it. Worldviews change the reality of what one perceives and responds to. Conflicts arise when worldviews collide and one person isn't able to let go of their notions or expectations built up by the perceptions they created over time. For example, Vegeta uses the Scouter's numbers to validate his own self-worth and invalidate others. He thinks of himself as the greatest and everyone else as worthless trash, *including* those who are more powerful because his father taught him that he is a superior being. Are they really trash, or is that label due to his perception?

Vegeta is the product of his environment. He was born a Saiya-jin and prone to ruthless fighting, but his upbringing made him even more violent, compassionless, selfish, and angry. These characteristics are evident throughout his entire life, and as he rises up he pushes others down in order to validate his own ego. A stark contrast to Goku.

2.3 GOKU'S PERSPECTIVE – EARTHLINGS AND INNER DEVELOPMENT

As full blooded Saiya-jins, Goku and Vegeta share similar genetic nature, but their environmental nurture is what separates them. How is this possible? Why is Goku so different?

Like Vegeta, Goku takes hardship as joy. He loves facing a strong opponent and pushing himself to surpass his limits. They both thrive in that environment. They crave it. But Goku has a childhood that completely changed his personality and worldview from that of a normal Saiya-jin, and particularly in contrast to Vegeta. Goku represents the opposite of everything that Vegeta stands for.

Consider that at birth, Kakarot (Goku's given name) was scientifically gauged by Scouter technology to have a battle power so low relative to other Saiya-jins that he was discarded altogether from their society. In *Dragon Ball Z: Bardock, The Father of Goku* TV Special (1990), a nursing ward technician says, "Yeah, he's definitely the kid of a lower class warrior. He's barely got any potential ability at all. The best we can do with him is send him off to one of the frontier planets." It's later shown in Bardock's Scouter that he has a power level of 2. This is why he was sent through space and landed on Earth. Kakarot was the last son of Planet Vegeta.

Think about this crucial scene for a moment. Kakarot was being placed into a Saiya-jin space pod so he could be sent to some far off planet. At the same time his father was single-handedly rebelling against Freeza and his men. Bardock's attack was futile, and as Freeza's massive *ki* ball ripped through his body, a sleeping baby blasted off the launch pad on his way to Earth. The *ki* ball landed on Planet Vegeta, penetrated its core, and catastrophically annihilated it, along with the entire Saiya-jin race. Bardock was killed and Planet Vegeta was gone, along with the Saiya-jin race. Vegeta was forced to experience the loss of his father, his planet and his people. Kakarot was a Saiya-jin but he knew nothing of what that meant. Kakarot's mind was empty, and because of that, it was able to be filled.

The child was adopted by an elderly martial arts master named Son Gohan who loved him as if he were his own. With his Saiya-jin nature the child was unusually powerful, uncontrollable, and wanted nothing to do with Son Gohan's kindness. One day while walking around the mountainside, the child pulled himself out of Son Gohan's makeshift baby basket as he reached for a fruit hanging on a tree branch, and fell into a deep ravine. He fell from such great heights that it would have killed a human child, but all he got was a nasty bump on the head. Even so, as a result of hitting his head on the hardened exposed roots of a tree he completely lost all knowledge of self. His rambunctious, violent Saiya-jin attitude was gone, replaced with a care free, wide eyed and happy go lucky mindset. "Grandpa" Gohan raised him up to the blue, empty sky, and seeing his big smiling face, decided to name him Son Goku (孫悟空)–A Buddhist name that means "The Child Aware of Emptiness."[3]

Goku is raised as an earthling and grows up in the wilderness atop Mt. Paozu, with only a small hermit hut as a home, which he shares with Gohan. Uneducated and simple minded, he knows little about technology and a lot about living in accordance with nature. He fishes with his hands and feet. He chops wood the same way. He avoids using external tools unless he has to and is completely unfamiliar with electronics. The first time he meets Bulma he thinks that she's a monster because she's inside a car. After she gets out, he then decides that the car is a monster and she's a witch.

Goku has a simple mindset because he lives in a simple, ancient way, far removed from the complications of society. The only technology he learns to use frequently is the Dragon Radar, and that's just so he can find the dragon balls. Goku is a feral child. A mountain boy. A country bumpkin with an accent.

Goku's character development is inspired by Eastern origins as a literary descendent of Sun Wukong (孫悟空) from *Journey to the West* (Chinese: *xīyóujì*, 西遊記, Japanese: *saiyūki*, 西遊記), a 16th century Chinese legend featuring Buddhist and Daoist belief systems. Goku's perspective is founded on the metaphysical beliefs of traditional East Asian culture: A respectful alignment with nature and faith in human potential. He is

---

3   Son Goku (孫悟空) can also be translated as "Grandson Awake to Vacuity," "Baby who Apprehends the Void," or "Young Boy Enlightened to Emptiness."

broad minded, compassionate and self-reliant because this is what those belief systems espouse. Buddha Law practices teach that all beings have "Buddha Nature." The Great Dao teachings express that all things are "One," and that as humans we are part of "The Way" and should live in accordance with nature. Goku becomes a product of this environment and lives these beliefs.

By nature Goku is a Saiya-jin, but by nurture he is a native earthling taught by hermit masters in traditional mind-body concepts and who grew up in the wild outdoors. Rather than use an external scientific device to harshly judge others, he is taught by kind hearted warriors to internally "feel" his opponents' subtle energy.

Goku learns to feel the energy of his opponents because he develops this skill while ascending the spiritual ladder with Son Gohan, Kame Sennin, Karin, Mister Popo, Kami and North Kaiō as his masters. It was gained through physical hardship combined with stillness in meditation. His true self is nurtured until the false self (the ego) is let go and his true self and the world unite. He can feel all living creatures, including the birds, fish, plants, other people and even planets. His mind is broad, and the concepts he was taught are totally different from the aliens who destroy anyone that doesn't comply with their notions and who grow up surrounded by scientific gadgets. Goku is a spiritual warrior because of the men who raised him.

2.3.1 BELIEVING BEFORE SEEING

Why is Goku taught this way? Because traditional East Asian self-cultivation practices teach that a normal person will only believe what they can see with their own two eyes while a supernormal person will believe it before they see it. Belief is a prerequisite to seeing. Because the normal person allows their eyes to be shrouded by the illusion of this physical world, they are blind to the truths at higher levels and won't believe in them. These people are said to have poor enlightenment quality (Chinese: *wùxìng*, 悟性), are lacking in wisdom, and are blind to the hidden potential inside all beings. The first character in *wùxìng* is also the first in

Goku's name (*wù* is pronounced *go* in Japanese), which symbolizes that Goku can perceive what others cannot.

The Western (or from a Japanese perspective, foreign) way of thinking is more externally accurate, with precise scientifically derived statistics independent of the situation, while the East Asian way of thinking is amorphous, with greater dependence on situational context. In such a paradigm the numbers and specifics become less important, with the emphasis instead on the intuitive nuances and emotion of the moment— the same way that it isn't absolutely necessary to be accurate when saying "It's over 9,000!" in real life when you mean "a lot." It's more about the feeling or heart of something rather than its precise external manifestation seen by the physical eyes.

Instead of relying on their own intuition and having compassion for others, these normal people rely on a set of external tools, whether that is the lenses of their own eyes or an additional external lens (such as the Scouter), to perceive the world. They only believe in quantifiable facts, the hard reality, and cannot see beyond themselves and their precious numbers. And that's because they're looking externally to begin with, and it's much easier to point the finger at someone or something else, instead of pointing inward.

As a Japanese author, Akira Toriyama writes to a Japanese audience and references East Asian culture. He makes the reader feel that Goku is the home team hero they should cheer for. To the Japanese readers Goku arguably appears Japanese, speaks with a countryside Japanese accent and his martial arts techniques are written in the more local and softer looking *hiragana* alphabet with occasional *kanji*. His association with legendary supernormal elements from the eastern fable *Journey to the West*, such as the Daoist magic cloud called *kinto'un* (English: Flying Nimbus), and his Buddhist magic staff, the *nyoi-bō* (English: Power Pole) strengthen this association. His insistence on referring to himself as Goku, a Japanese Buddhist name given to him on Earth, while Vegeta insists on calling him Kakarot, a name given to him on Planet Vegeta, strengthens this association even further. Goku is the modern illustrated personification of thousands of years of traditional East Asian culture, embodied as one character.

Goku is a native earthling while Vegeta is a foreign alien. To make the dichotomy even more apparent, Toriyama differentiates their clothing (Goku wears traditional martial arts uniform while Vegeta wears advanced battle armor) and hair (Goku's hair is broad while Vegeta's is straight up). To the Japanese, foreign terms, including those transliterated from English, are usually written in *katakana*. Toriyama further emphasizes the difference by writing most of Vegeta's techniques in the *katakana* alphabet, derived from English, such as Final Flash (Japanese: *Fainaru Furasshu*, ファイナルフラッシュ), and Big Bang Attack (Japanese: *Biggu Ban Atakku*, ビッグバンアタック). Likewise Scouters (Japanese: *Sukautā*, スカウター) and their Saiya-jin names, Vegeta (Japanese: *Bejīta*, ベジータ) and Kakarot (Japanese: *Kakarotto*, カカロット).

Most importantly, Goku is taught to believe in the potential of others before he sees their potential realized while Vegeta is taught to believe that no one has potential and should be killed when no longer useful. Goku believes before he sees, which becomes a quintessential aspect of his character.

2.3.2 DYNAMIC AND BROAD ENERGY – NOT STATIC

One of the fundamental differences between the warriors on Earth and the aliens abroad is that the earthlings do not have a fixed power level. It is dynamic rather than static.

This difference is extremely important to understand. On Earth, people have limitless potential and can become whatever they want. Anyone can learn to cultivate their *ki*, it is only a matter of the proper knowledge and disciplined application of principles. There are those stronger than others, but fixed values don't exist. Their power is only gauged in relationship to another being's actions, not by an external reading, because a being's genuine power level cannot be known until it is expressed. With the right training poor peasants can be stronger than rich elites. Later in the series, even the gods are in awe of the power that Goku, Gohan and the others put out in brief moments of intense activity.

If we can compare the two type of *ki* training through the analogy of electronic devices, then the energy of earthlings functions like an analog volume knob in that there are gradations of quiet or loud over a wide range. Through martial arts training the energy can be mentally restrained or increased much higher than normal during fits of emotional rage. In contrast, the alien's power levels are like a digital button, in that the number is set to a specific point and there is no fluctuation.

On Earth it is a given that each person is born with potential for greatness. Some have a higher amount of potential than others (what Daoist's call "Inborn Quality") and some learn faster than others (what Buddhist's call (the aforementioned) "Enlightenment Quality"), but everyone has the ability to tap into their potential. The more they train, the deeper their spiritual well goes, and it's up to them how much energy they want to draw forth. They can either go shallow or deep. At times they draw energy from so deep within the well that it causes a substantial change of consciousness. For those with incredibly deep potential, the well can extend further and further down before reaching the ultimate limit. For the earthlings, expressing their *ki* is a matter of self-control–either using it or letting it go.

The aliens' energy cannot go higher than their power level limit without a transformational change in body type or further training after the battle. In this sense the aliens are like living representations of the technology they surround themselves with and wear on their bodies. They *are* what they *use* because that is their mindset. The aliens have very high power levels by default, stronger than most humans, but they don't know how to increase or reduce their *ki* during a battle unless it's through physical transformation in which their body actually changes shape, thus altering the compositional balance of their overall energy. For the aliens it's only a matter of how to utilize the power they already have with each attack to the maximum extent. And this is strange because they all *have* potential, just as the earthlings do, but their society is so different that they don't learn how to tap into it.

There are exceptions, but for the most part the earthlings have kindness. They have compassion for others, rely on their friends, communicate and share one another's suffering to help bear the burden. They may be defeated in one-on-one fights, such as when Yamcha loses his life to a suicide attack against a Saibaman, but they can team up to take on stronger opponents and win the day. For example, if the "Z Warriors" had not collaborated against Nappa and Vegeta to buy time for Goku's return to Earth, then he might not have had a world to defend.

There's no way Goku could have won the battle against Vegeta without his friends. Despite his incredible training he truly was outclassed. He still won because a man's power level is not the only deciding factor in the outcome of a fight. That's true whether it's an external battle for life or death, or an internal struggle to overcome a personal demon. There are too many hidden variables that a Scouter cannot detect.

2.3.3 HE WHO CONQUERS HIMSELF

The Daoist patriarch Laozi is credited with saying, "He who conquers others is strong. He who conquers himself is mighty." Simply put, Goku fights to improve himself and raise his abilities because it makes him feel stronger and happy. He has internal confidence and doesn't care about power levels. He doesn't need a number to validate his own self-worth. Goku seeks stronger opponents to push himself farther and prove that he is stronger than he was before, not to validate his own existence and invalidate theirs, as Vegeta does.

Generally speaking, the villainous characters want to be better than everyone else, while the good natured characters just want to be better than themselves. Of course not all of the good guys start out that way. Many of them are selfish in the beginning, but the more time they spend around Goku the more they change. By the end of the series, the majority align themselves with Goku's perspective and become spiritual warriors just like him. And why not? Without his selfless actions they wouldn't even be alive. Most importantly, Goku is the one striving for *self*-superiority and he is the one who truly achieves it. All of the others improve and learn more about themselves because they're trying to catch up to him.

Goku's life runs counter to Saiya-jin culture. Goku is hopeful that others can change, and that's because he himself is a person who changes! It's in-character for him to offer hope and redemption, because he first offers hope and redemption to himself. He wouldn't rise up as quickly as he did if he didn't think that way. He is as Vegeta described in *Dragon Ball Z* episode 280, "a kind-hearted Saiya-jin."

Thus, Goku is the manifest opposite of what Vegeta believes Saiya-jin culture and its people represent. To Vegeta, Goku's very existence is a slap in the face and an insult to his pride, the source of his strength.

And that is why they clash.

2.4 VEGETA CLASHES WITH OTHERS

Vegeta's clashes with others are about telling the story of his personal development. His battles before Goku have little meaning except to demonstrate his desire to dominate over others. However, his battle with Goku and those after Goku mark a shift in his story. His worldview starts to crumble away, piece by piece, forever changing his character and providing one of the most interesting personality changes in the history of anime. The moment Vegeta screamed "It's over 9,000!" and broke that Scouter is the moment his life began to change.

Through successive battles he goes from a proud, egotistical, Scouter reliant man like any other in the Freeza Empire, to humiliated and vengeful. Finally letting go of his Scouter, Vegeta learns to rely on his own intuition and inner strength to enact revenge. At every step he breaks down another mental wall built up to protect himself, and by doing so he taps into more potential and increases his power level.

The battle between Goku and Vegeta changed both their lives. To see how, we have to look at what Vegeta was like before the two actually made physical contact.

Remember that Goku had just broken Nappa's spine and paralyzed him from the waist down. What does Vegeta do with his partner and fellow Saiya-jin, a man who helped raise and protect him? A man who understood him better than anyone?

He kills him!

He picks Nappa up by the hand, flings him into the sky, and hits him with a *ki* blast that causes his body to explode into nothingness. That's how little Vegeta cared for Nappa. He saw Nappa as a tool that performed his bidding, and when that tool was exhausted he threw it out like a piece of trash. Vegeta did this because according to his mindset Nappa no longer had any value and might as well be discarded. Freeza set the precedent of treating others this way and Vegeta followed it.

Suffice to say that Vegeta loses the fight against Goku and his friends, not because of a lack in power, ability, or intensity. Rather because he lacks insight and can't see past himself. He judges Goku and says that he's "low class" trash. He relies on the Scouter to validate his own superiority. He kills his own partner after standing on the sidelines and letting him do all the preliminary work. Vegeta is very much like Sun Wukong from *Journey to the West*, in that he gladly fights alone against superior numbers, filled with pride and the belief that he is stronger than the gods, more powerful than the "Will of Heaven" and even the Buddha. Sun Wukong is the character Son Goku is named after, but Vegeta inherited his cocky attitude.

Vegeta's fight against Goku represents a collision of external scientific technology versus internal spiritual beliefs, class versus classless, and individualism versus relationships. Despite Vegeta's strengths, his internal character flaws cause him to lose the fight all the same, and it's because the earthlings had spiritual warrior training, didn't think in terms of class, and worked together as friends.

At the end of the fight Vegeta crawls away as a bloody mess and tries to climb into his Saiya-jin space pod. Krillin holds Yajirobe's katana to Vegeta's face and is about to deliver the death blow.

But Goku stops him.

Goku *chooses* to keep Vegeta alive! He does this despite the fact that Vegeta and Nappa were in the process of killing his son, just killed some of his best friends, attempted to annihilate the Earth, and crushed every bone in his own body. Goku lets all of that go. He sees past it, and looks at the positive aspects of Vegeta's character, the parts that he admires.

Goku's choice gave Vegeta the time he needed to change his worldview. Vegeta didn't realize it at first, and he tried to fight against it, but the more time Vegeta spent nearby Goku or within his circle, the more he changed.

2.4.1 THE EVOLVING EYES OF A SUPER ELITE

Vegeta changes after fighting Goku. The first of these many changes was his newfound ability to look within, to have insight and the intuitive ability to control and sense power levels *without* a Scouter.

Perhaps because he was faced with an overwhelming case of reality in the form of defeat, Vegeta makes the decision to change and grow. He lets go of his reliance on the external Scouter and instead relies on his own internal ability. He's still a ruthless murderer, mind you, but he has gained the ability to regulate his power. This is the sole reason why he survives as long as he does on Planet Namek. If he took the easier way out and chose to stay the same as the other aliens, then he would have continued to see the world in the same light that they do.

Let's take a moment to examine Vegeta's life after Goku.

So Vegeta had just lost the fight and escaped in his Saiya-jin space pod. He lands on Planet Freeza 79 at a military base, where his wounds are healed. He learns that Freeza has traveled to Planet Namek to gather the dragon balls and wish for immortality. Vegeta becomes furious and chases after him so he can gather the dragon balls first and wish for his own immortality, thus gaining the power to enact sweet revenge.

Vegeta initially still uses the Scouter out of old habit, but quickly lets it go after realizing just how talented he really is. The proof he needed came in the form of an old rival within the Freeza Empire, named Kui, who likewise chased Vegeta to Planet Namek in order to kill him. They had a longstanding rivalry.

After landing, Kui locates Vegeta with his Scouter and flies to his location. Because Kui believes his power level is superior, he issues a challenge.

Kui: "How do you expect to win with a power of your size?"

Vegeta: "Hahaha. You rely on your Scouter too much."

Kui: "Pff! What is that supposed to mean?"

Vegeta: "It means I've learned to control my power!!!" *Vegeta powers up.* "Look at my power level with your Scouter now!"

Kui: "Impossible! It's as high as mine!" *Kui becomes terrified as the number increases rapidly.*

Vegeta establishes his supremacy and the number, all by itself, is enough to make Kui take back his death threat and instead offer an alliance against Freeza. But Vegeta is not so easily fooled. As Kui flies away for his life, Vegeta points two fingers at him and makes him explode.

The numbers derived from the Scouter can be inspiring or terrifying depending on who perceives them. We see a similar scenario when Vegeta encounters Dodoria, one of Freeza's personal bodyguards and henchmen. Dodoria, like the other aliens, judges Vegeta based on his power level and dismisses him outright. But Vegeta surprises Dodoria because his power level increased a great deal after his near-death experience with Goku.

Dodoria's Scouter had recently been broken in a conflict with the Namek-sei-jins (the people of Planet Namek), so he asks Vegeta for his Scouter, but Vegeta takes it off, drops it on the ground, and stomps it to pieces.

Dodoria: "What are you doing Vegeta?! Have you gone crazy? Why did you break it?"

Vegeta: "I don't need it."

Dodoria: "What?! Didn't you want the dragon balls? Without that, you can't find Freeza or the Namek-sei-jins!"

> **Vegeta:** "On Earth I learned that certain earthlings had the ability to locate and measure *ki* without a Scouter. A Saiya-jin who lived on Earth had the same power, so why not me?"
>
> **Dodoria:** "..."
>
> **Vegeta:** "I just have to learn that trick. For someone like yourself who only counts on power, it would be impossible to master the ability. I used to be like you."

Dodoria becomes outraged that Vegeta is more powerful than he is and refuses to accept it. He screams, "The number was wrong! The Scouter was broken, that's all! Don't mock me!!" Vegeta then defeats Dodoria in combat and frightens him into providing valuable information. Most importantly the true cause of the Saiya-jin annihilation. That it wasn't a "meteor" that destroyed Planet Vegeta on accident. It was a purposeful genocide by Freeza!

Instead of being shocked at the revelation, Vegeta says that he doesn't really care about the death or loss of his people. What he cares about is how they were *manipulated* by Freeza and made to be his *servants*. It's his Saiya-jin *pride* that is wounded. And as Dodoria flies away in fear, Vegeta once again kills his opponent. This time with a huge *ki* blast.

So you can already see that Vegeta changes his perspective by letting go of the Scouter, but he's still a very proud and stubborn killer. It's also around this point that he begins to mention the Legendary Super Saiya-jin, a being that is said to be more powerful than all others in the universe, and which even Freeza himself is terrified of encountering. Vegeta mentions it because he believes that *he is* the Legendary Super Saiya-jin reborn, and his absolute supremacy will be displayed on the battlefield and experienced by his opponents. He believes this because his father told him that he among all Saiya-jins had the most likely chance of fulfilling the legend, and that it was his right as the Prince.

Vegeta mentions the Legendary Super Saiya-jin again and again, in all of his battles, and to Goku as well after he finally makes it to Namek. He continuously validates his own power and belief system that *he* is the

Legendary Super Saiya-jin. The legend fuses into his own mentality and combines with his already enormous pride to become the will that keeps him going.

But what's most interesting is that Vegeta's confidence wavers back and forth during his life story. He always *sounds* tough and hard, but really his ego is like an extremely fragile house of cards that is often dependent upon his own self-worth in the eyes of others. When he's above their power level he feels confident and strong. When he's below their power level he feels frustrated and motivated to get back on top. Sometimes even afraid or defeated. He's so competitive that he would rather train to the point of near death (and then barely survive and subsequently power up) than be content that there's someone better out there.

The next person on Vegeta's hit list was Zarbon, Freeza's right-hand-man. When Vegeta is fighting Zarbon they go through the same song and dance as with Dodoria. Zarbon had seen the higher number on his Scouter previously and was slightly surprised, but not terrified. Nevertheless, Vegeta believes that his power is superior to Zarbon's and begins beating him down.

But then Zarbon transforms into his more powerful "ugly" version, causing his power level to increase dramatically, and Vegeta suffers a near fatal defeat. Vegeta could sense the power increase after Zarbon's transformation but was helpless to do anything but hold on for his life. He's knocked into the sea and left for dead as Zarbon returns to Freeza to report the good news.

Vegeta gains an increase in power after recovering from his near death experience. Filled with confidence he goes to fight Zarbon again. Zarbon meets him half way because he was ordered by Freeza to bring back Vegeta's body as proof. This time Zarbon thinks that Vegeta is a complete fool. Didn't he just lose? But Vegeta relies on his own intuition and senses to gauge his opponent's strength. Lo and behold Vegeta now has a higher power level than Zarbon does. The end result is that Zarbon is scared, gets a fist through his stomach and a hole blown through his back with a *ki* blast.

Vegeta fights his way across Namek and faces multiple foes such as the Ginyu Tokusentai (English: Ginyu Force), Freeza's super elite strike squad. After several other battles occur, a similar event to the above scenarios happens while he battles Jeice. Jeice is a member of the Ginyu Tokusentai and believes he is superior to all of the Saiya-jins. And why shouldn't he? The Scouter has shown the same number time and time again. Vegeta tells Jeice to check his Scouter one more time, and yep, you guessed it, Vegeta has a higher power level than he does. Jeice becomes frightened for his life specifically because of this number and Vegeta evaporates him with a giant *ki* blast. Vegeta then goes on to defeat Captain Ginyu himself.

Why is all of this important? Because what you're witnessing across this arc of the story is Vegeta's transcendence as a man over his former suppressors. The people that tried to keep him down through their own elitist mentalities were conquered by an even *more* elitist attitude and an even *stronger* sense of pride. The difference between them is that Vegeta began to rely on his own internal power, rather than the Scouter, and he actually used the psychology of the Scouter numbers *against* his opponents as if it were a weakness to exploit. Because that's exactly what it was, and it's the reason, along with Vegeta's incredible fortitude, that he was able to win so many fights.

After years of living underneath Freeza's heel and planning his revenge, Vegeta now feels that he's strong enough to take on the overlord. But after a long and drawn out struggle, it turns out that no, he is not. Vegeta does not wish for immortality. He does not become the Legendary Super Saiya-jin he believed in so strongly. He does not defeat Freeza.

Instead, Vegeta dies from a *ki* blast to the heart after emptying his soul to Goku and tearfully telling his story of a life of servitude. The proud, Saiya-jin prince, cries before a "low class" discard and passes his will of vengeance onto him.

Vegeta is without a doubt a stubborn man, but when he took that *ki* blast to the heart it represented more than a physical death. A part of his very reason for living was given to another. Luckily for Vegeta, Krillin, Gohan and Dende gather the dragon balls and wish him back to life (along with all of the other people killed by Freeza and his men) while Goku battles Freeza. Vegeta dies and is then *born again* before being teleported to

Earth via another wish. In many ways Vegeta's former self died when his heart was pierced, only to be reborn a new man with a new perspective. He just didn't realize it yet.

Having been teleported to Earth, Vegeta has the understanding that both Freeza and Goku died during the explosion of Planet Namek, and that he is now the most powerful being in the universe. With his greatest enemy and newfound rival dead he is forced to find a new source of motivation. Yet with no one to fight he starts to become comfortable on Earth, going so far as to call it his home. When Goku's family and friends try to wish Goku back to life they find out that *he is alive after all*, somewhere in outer space!

Vegeta's motivation returns. His goal? Become more powerful than Goku!!

2.4.2 LOSS AND GAIN

Vegeta's philosophical transformation that started with Goku comes full circle. It was through battling Goku and the earthlings that Vegeta was forced to grow. He expanded his inner potential by looking within to navigate the world instead of depending on an external and limiting device.

There is no gain without loss, and Vegeta experienced firsthand that when you lose externally you gain internally. In the Saiya-jin Saga he lost his tail and suffered a blow to his pride, but gained insight. In the Namek Saga he lost the Scouter and suffered physical agony, but gained the power to defeat his oppressors. In the Freeza Saga he is forced to tears in front of the lowest of the lows (Kakarot), pleading for vengeance. He hits rock bottom and then dies, having lost all that he could. What did he gain? A physical and spiritual re-awakening. A new chance at life.

Vegeta goes through a fundamental change after experiencing death and rebirth. Having already lost the external, he now begins to lose internally, letting go of his own mental constructs and attachments over the course of the series. He gains spiritual ascension, and in his own way a strange sense of acceptance. Vegeta fights against it at every step. He is always looking for ways to improve, as this is a quintessential aspect of who he is, but he does it while trying to reclaim his pride and his original ego-driven ways. In the process he almost causes the end of the entire universe while fighting both Cell and Majin Buu! But once again as a result of his rivalry with Goku he ultimately enlightens to his own inner truths.

Vegeta finally understands the reality of who he is and his place in the world. He becomes an earthling, starts a family with Bulma, and attains, in some sense, peace. Were it not for his strong will and constant desire to be the best, he could have enjoyed it. But then again, that's what makes Vegeta who he is.

So what is the lesson? Perhaps that we should have compassion for Vegeta and try to understand the internal struggles that he goes through, because it's the same struggles that we all go through in life in trying to validate our existence, just exaggerated to a *Dragon Ball Z* extreme.

Toriyama is also giving the reader a moral lesson through Vegeta's actions. In the same way that Vegeta takes off his own Scouter, we should all take off our own invisible Scouters and let notions and judgments fall away so that we can grow. Otherwise we will be limited by old concepts and fear based illusions.

Vegeta represents the part of man that always wants to be better and will not stop until it is achieved. The all-powerful will that rises up against the challenges that serve to keep us down.

Vegeta inspires. That is why he is so adored by fans across the world.

Now let's take a look at Goku's worldview and see how his conflicts cause his character in the *Dragon Ball* story to grow.

2.5 GOKU CHANGES THOSE AROUND HIM

Goku is a force of change, both in himself and others. And sometimes Goku is the harbinger of change while other times he is the one forced to adapt. His fight against Vegeta is just one of many instances where conflict comes to Goku unwillingly. He wasn't asking for trouble. Trouble came to him. The resulting conflicts not only force him to change, but his opponents too.

By the end of the original *Dragon Ball* the conflicts on Earth had mostly been settled. Piccolo was still lurking about, but Goku had already proven that he was the better man. Who else was there to fight?

Starting the rest of his life, Goku marries Chi-Chi and has a son, named Gohan in honor of his grandpa. There's peace on Earth for the next 5 years, until that one fateful day.

2.5.1 GOKU MEETS RADITZ! THE VIOLENT CLASH BEGINS! RADITZ DIES!! GOKU DIES!!

Goku's life drastically changes when his long lost brother Raditz decides to have a family reunion. Suffice to say that Goku does not enjoy his first experience being quantified by the Scouter, nor the treatment that his brother gives him as a result. Goku and Raditz are genetically similar, but just as with Vegeta, their upbringing and mentality are worlds apart. Because of this, there are conflicts.

When Raditz arrives on Earth the very first thing he does is check his Scouter to examine the power of the farmer and determine whether or not the citizens of this planet are a threat. With the farmer's power level of 5, he determines they're not. He then checks for other large power sources around the planet. He finds Piccolo instead of Goku, and after being hit by Piccolo's *ki* blast determines that Piccolo is so weak it's not even worth the time to kill him. He locates Goku and flies to his location on Kame Island.

Change comes whether you like it or not, and in this case it came hard and fast. Raditz condemns Goku as weak and soft, ridiculing the fact that he no longer has a tail, the very symbol that makes him a Saiya-jin. In the Viz Media English edition of *Dragon Ball Z* manga volume 17, Raditz explains their family heritage:

Raditz: "That is because you and I... We are the *same*!! You are no earthling! You are a Saiya-jin warrior... A member of the most powerful race in the universe!!"

Goku: "Shut up!! I don't care if you *are* my brother! I don't care if I *am* an alien!! Krillin was right... People like you are just *wrong*!! I'm Son Goku now!! Get th'heck off my planet!!"

Bulma: "You tell 'im Goku!"

Kame Sennin: "Nurture over nature, m'boy! Goku's not just an *earthling*... He's th'best dang earthling I know!"

Krillin: "He even *saved* this planet once! So do us a favor an' just *go*, will ya!?"

Raditz provokes him further, knees him in the stomach and then kidnaps his son, Gohan. He gives Goku an ultimatum.

Option 1: Kill 100 people of Earth and pile the bodies on this Island.

Option 2: Your son will be murdered.

Raditz says, "If you wish him returned to you *alive*, Kakarot... You will follow my orders... Is that clear? Do it and we fly off together to pile up a few million more bodies. Fail, and there'll be only one dead body... your sons."

Raditz's behavior and reliance on the Scouter shows how the Saiya-jins navigate through life. They use external technology to judge others and guide their self serving decisions. This turns out to be the cause of Raditz's downfall because he did not expect Goku or Piccolo to chase after him together. He did not expect Gohan to strike him in the chest with a rage powered flying head butt. He did not expect Piccolo's *makankōsappō* (Japanese: 魔貫光殺砲, English: Special Beam Cannon) to be capable of such power.

Why not? Because in his mind, Piccolo, Goku, and Gohan all had a *static* power level. Raditz died as a result of his reliance on the Scouter for the same reasons the aliens died on Namek when fighting Vegeta when he chose to go without one.

Goku dies as well from Piccolo's technique, but it was a willing sacrifice. That was his choice and it's one that saved the planet. As a result he goes to the Other World, trains with North Kaiō in *kaiō ken* (Japanese: 界王拳) martial arts and learns the *genki dama* (Japanese: 元気玉, English: Spirit Bomb) technique.

A year later Goku rushes back to Earth to fight against Nappa and Vegeta.

2.5.2 IT'S OVER 9,000?! IMPOSSIBLE!!

When Goku arrived to the battlefield, the way that Vegeta knew was because an indicator flashed on his Scouter. He looked up, and sure enough, Goku was there. Krillin, Gohan and Piccolo had sensed Goku's arrival from miles away.

Like Raditz, Vegeta checked Goku's power level and determined that he was disappointingly weak and not worth waiting for. Goku powered up in rage over his fallen comrades, and we are led into the now famous Over 9,000 scene, where both Nappa and Vegeta are shocked.

Goku was classified as a "low class" Saiya-jin like his father Bardock before him, but Goku was unaware of this classification. The concept never entered his mind that he wasn't good enough, so he was never limited by it. Both Nappa and Vegeta try to place the limit on Goku.

In *Dragon Ball Z* episode 30, Nappa has been killed by Vegeta and now both he and Goku face off in the barren wasteland. They stand on top of cliffs with a great divide between them. Vegeta stands on a higher cliff than Goku and tells him exactly how he feels:

> **Vegeta:** "Saiya-jins have their power levels examined right after they are born. The scum that have lower ratings, such as yourself, are sent off to planets that do not have terribly formidable opponents. In other

words... You were a left-behind!"

Goku: "And as a result, I was sent to Earth, here? I should be thankful. But what's more... Even a left-behind might be able to overcome an elite, if he tries desperately enough."

Vegeta: "Hehehe. An amusing joke." *Vegeta smirks.* "Now then, allow me to show you a barrier that you cannot overcome, no matter how hard you try!"

Goku is unmoved by Vegeta's words. He replies with a smile and a *kaiō ken* powered punch to the face.

How could Goku possibly have a power level over 9,000? That's what Nappa and Vegeta try to wrap their heads around. It goes against everything they believe about themselves and their place in the world. Goku says repeatedly that they should just stop fighting and go home, but of course they don't listen. They're forced to change the hard way because Goku doesn't mess around when it comes to life and death, especially when other people's lives are on the line.

Goku has a power level of over 9,000 (over 8,000 in the original Japanese) because he worked hard at it. He purposefully died, ran over 1 million kilometers (10,000 miles in the FUNimation dub) across Snake Way and trained on 10 times Earth's normal gravity with a *god* for months of intense, focused and disciplined martial arts cultivation, and *then* he flew back across Snake Way so he could make it in time for the battle.

If that's not hard work, then what is?

Goku tolerated no distractions and was completely focused on his training and the challenge at hand. He changed that quickly because he sacrificed, endured and went the distance.

When you lose, you gain. So what did he gain?

Everything else! He gained the ability to endure tremendous suffering. He gained the ability to speak with the planet and all beings, animate or inanimate. And he gained the strength and techniques necessary to survive a battle with his greatest foe to date. He gained all of that because he let go of his ego and fought to defeat himself. His battle with Vegeta was really a test to see if he could overcome his own physical and mental limitations, and that's why Goku was so excited to fight him.

In the end, Vegeta was forced to flee. "Never... Never before... Have I had to *retreat...*" he says. Vegeta crawls into his space pod, closes the hatch and blasts off. Goku's crushed body is incapable of moving, but he has friends who care. Bulma and company arrive in their air-van and pick Goku up to go to the hospital.

2.5.3 MINDS AND BODIES

Goku's mind becomes so broad and expansive after his recovery from the fight with the Saiya-jins and his subsequent training on board the spaceship to Planet Namek that he could sense and *see* every living being on the planet.

He arrives on Namek, comes out of his space ship and is able to see all the people *in his mind*. He can actually see them. His sight has gone beyond sight. Forget Scouters. Goku can see everything with such clarity within his own mind that using a Scouter would be a hindrance.

Goku gains this ability through not only his incredible training, but by improving his character and his ability to endure. It's an internal mind-body science that cultivated this ability, and it's something that no one else ever gains, despite undergoing similar training with North Kaiō. So it's not just about achieving a high power level, it's about the unique quality of Goku's character. This ability goes wherever he goes, doesn't require electricity and can't be broken. In Buddha Law cultivation practices it is called the Heavenly Eye (Chinese: *tiānmù*, 天目, Japanese: *tenme*, 天目), or commonly called the Third Eye, as is physically present on Tenshinhan's forehead in *Dragon Ball*.

Goku immediately flies to Gohan's location where he, Krillin and Vegeta are about to die fighting the Ginyu Tokusentai. He then uses another newfound ability to read Krillin's mind and determine what occurred in the past. Goku places his hand on top of Krillin's head and uses retrocognition to *see* the events unfold in his own mind. He sees the battles they endured, and everything else. How is that possible? Because according to the traditional East Asian beliefs that *Dragon Ball* is inspired by, everything that occurs in the universe leaves an image and message in time. If the supernormal ability of retrocognition is unlocked, then a person can see past events and the history of other living beings. It's as clear as if you were looking at it directly, and using this ability Goku is instantly brought up to speed without the need for words.

As usual the Ginyu Tokusentai members use the Scouter to determine Goku's power level and then judge his worth. Unfortunately for them, Goku was suppressing his true power. Goku soundly defeats Recoome and Burter with a single blow each. The only ones left are Jeice (whom Vegeta later kills) and Captain Ginyu.

Toriyama uses these quick battles to show Goku's progress while training aboard the spaceship on his way to Namek, and how far he has surpassed Vegeta, who was on the verge of death. He then goes even further beyond by facing off with the leader, Captain Ginyu.

Ginyu, like all of Freeza's men, is reliant on the Scouter, however he is unique because while he uses the Scouter just like everyone else, he's experienced enough to know there are beings in the galaxy capable of hiding and drawing forth their power on command, just like Vegeta learned how to do. Ginyu says, "You're still hiding your real power! You think I don't feel it? I have the ability to change my power at will too."

Out of curiosity he offers Goku the chance to power up to his maximum, also offering the viewer at home the chance to see just how quantifiably more powerful Goku has become since his battle with Vegeta. Goku powers up and the number on his Scouter rises up to 180,000! *Way* over 9,000. Ginyu screams, "Impossible! It's still rising! I can't believe it!" He completely freaks out. "That's your real power?"

Ginyu is so amazed at Goku's power level that he decides to *take* Goku's body using his mind-change technique, where he physically transfers his own consciousness out of his current body and into the target body, while pulling the target's consciousness into his current body. The way Ginyu does this is by looking his opponent straight in the eyes (the window to the soul) and forming a connection, and then firing some kind of energetic beam that makes physical contact with the subject and creates a circuitous bridge. The consciousness of the two people are swapped like two ends of a pole being reversed along a straight line. It's an amazing concept and very spiritually and physically thought provoking. It may also explain why Ginyu is different from the other aliens and can control his power level like the earthlings and Namek-sei-jins. He's more in touch with his own consciousness and the mind-body connection, whichever body that may be.

While inhabiting Goku's body Captain Ginyu returns to Freeza's ship where Gohan and Krillin are standing next to the 7 dragon balls. Ginyu is wearing his Scouter because it's habitual for him to do so, and this is one of the ways that the earthlings recognize that "Goku" isn't really Goku. The Scouter is the *symbol* that they're aliens. Gohan quickly senses the evil *ki* in Ginyu's energy and then Ginyu slaps Krillin in the face and they start to fight.

While Ginyu is more sensitive to the mind-body connection than the other aliens, in the end the body change doesn't work out for Ginyu. He doesn't fully understand how to do what Goku and other earthlings do, and can't draw out all of the power in Goku's body. That's because it's not just about the physical body. It's about the power of the consciousness *within* the body that has trained and grown *with that body*. The mind-body connection is fundamentally important, and the earthlings *purposefully* trained to strengthen this connection, something the aliens never did. Ginyu had talent but he lacked the necessary worldview.

In an odd twist, Vegeta ends up beating the life out of Goku's body while Ginyu inhabits it. Vegeta knows he is fighting Ginyu so he takes no pride in having defeated "Goku," because he really didn't. Their rivalry is about the internal consciousnesses and personalities fighting one another. The external bodies are secondary. That said, after the fight is over and Goku gets his original body back, he has to spend some time in the recovery chamber aboard Freeza's ship before fighting the man himself.

When Goku exits the chamber (with not a second to spare, mind you), he has arguably the most challenging opponent of his life waiting outside to meet him.

2.5.4 THE SUPER SAIYA-JIN WILL

Goku stands before a broken man. Vegeta lies in the dirt, pouring out his heart and soul, trying to pass his will and Saiya-jin pride onto the last surviving Saiya-jin, the one he calls Kakarot. The one he believes will fulfill the Super Saiya-jin legend in his place. Not too far away stands Freeza, the overlord who controlled Vegeta's entire life.

Goku doesn't understand what Vegeta and the other aliens have been talking about with all this "Super Saiya-jin" stuff, but to Vegeta it's extremely important, and he goes on and on about it. Why? Because it's why Freeza was afraid and implemented power level judgments at birth. It's why the Saiya-jins were wiped out. *It's why Vegeta struggles so hard.* If Vegeta can become a Super Saiya-jin then he'll be the strongest in the universe and can *enact his revenge*. It's everything he wants in life.

In the Viz Media English edition of *Dragon Ball Z* manga volume 26, Vegeta struggles to breathe and knows that he is dying:

> **Vegeta:** "Ka... Kakarot... You're still too naïve... too much to be... to be a Super Saiya-jin! B... Be... heartless and cold blooded! Yes... you could become a Super Saiya-jin... if you were more *realistic!*"

> **Goku:** "I can't be heartless like you, and... I didn't understand all your story about the Super Saiya-jins."

> **Vegeta:** "L... Listen well, Kakarot. Planet Vegeta, our mother planet... wasn't destroyed by an asteroid..."

> **Freeza:** "I pierced a hole through his heart... still, he keeps talking?"

> **Vegeta:** "It... It's Freeza who destroyed it. Us Saiya-jins were slaves to him! Except for us they were all exterminated. Your parents, my father, the king... all that because Freeza was afraid of Super Saiya-jins."

> **Freeza:** "Hmph! What's he talking about?"

Finally with his last breath Vegeta reaches the extreme opposite of his prideful nature.

Vegeta: "I... I beg of you! Eliminate Freeza!! Please...! He must die... from the hands... of a Saiya-jin."

The Prince of all Saiya-jins passes away.

Goku: "Vegeta!!!"

Freeza: "He's dead? Not a moment too soon! Can we continue our horrid show?"

Goku takes a moment to give Vegeta a proper burial and continues speaking while laying him into the ground. He says, "You cried. You asked me a favor. I can imagine your rage. It wasn't because all the Saiya-jins died. I get it. You're regretful you were manipulated by Freeza. I hated you, but I must admit you were worthy of the Saiya-jin name. I will follow your advice."

Goku stands up and faces Freeza:

Goku: "I was raised on Earth, but I'm also a Saiya-jin! For all the Saiya-jins and Namek-sei-jin's you killed... I will defeat you!!"

Freeza: "Stop saying such stupid things!"

Goku throws the first punch.

It marks the beginning of a lengthy and grand battle.

2.5.5 BROAD MINDED VISION AND NARROW MINDED VISION

While Goku is broad minded (or naïve, as Vegeta refers to it), Freeza and the other Scouter users are narrow minded. This is a reflection of their worldviews, either with broad vision or narrow vision. These two ways of looking at the world determine the choices they make because broad minded vision is inclusive while narrow minded vision is divisive.

The key thing about Freeza's worldview is that not only does he come with a Scouter, after his Scouter and henchmen's Scouter's are destroyed, he asks the Ginyu Tokusentai for *more*. He *needs* a Scouter and is handicapped without it. Goku is so broad minded that he can see a being just by thinking about them, like the powerful spiritual warrior that he is. Even though he's on top of the social pyramid he created and should have the widest vision, Freeza's vision is just as narrow mindedly limited by the Scouter as everyone else's.

The aliens used an external mechanical science to develop the Scouters rather than internal mind-body science, and without the Scouters they are at a disadvantage. While Freeza's fighting against Goku amid the smoke and dust of Namek, he is unable to see his opponent. Goku can sense Freeza's presence no matter where he goes, but Freeza can't. He blindly fires eye beams into the clouds of dust, completely missing Goku. Goku enlightens to this and controls the fight with Freeza for a while. Of course Freeza retaliates by utilizing more of his power, and the violent dance continues.

Freeza judges Goku throughout the battle just like the other aliens beforehand. He calls Goku a monkey, mocks his low power level while validating his own, toys around with Goku and generally treats him like a piece of garbage. Goku is broad minded, tolerant and enduring, but he has limits like everyone else. Goku endures again and again until Freeza finally pushes him over the edge.

Freeza kills Goku's best friend, Krillin.

Everything falls away. Goku let's go of all of his attachments. His naturally broad mind reaches the opposite extreme. His eyes and eyebrows change from curved and open to angular and squinted. Anger causes his mind to become so narrow that the only thing left is a singular rage directed entirely at Freeza.

Goku completely lets go of his restraints and gives into the anger. Dark clouds fill the sky and lightning arcs across the battle damaged planet. Goku's consciousness, now free of the weights of his concern for others, rises up, draws forth hidden energy from the well of his consciousness and *explodes* in a golden fire and light. His hair turns golden, the pupils in his eyes vanish (symbolizing the loss of control over his consciousness, and giving into a sub-conscious Saiya-jin rage), he screams in transcendental pain as the energy deep inside his mind and body is unlocked, reaches the surface and pours out! Goku becomes the Legendary Super Saiya-jin!!

Goku is the one.

His pupils return as he regains control of his mind, only now they are a greenish-blue color, rather than black. With a stern appearance he looks at Gohan and tells him to "Leave, now!" It's time for revenge against Freeza for all those he killed, including Vegeta.

Goku screams at Freeza, "No more! NO MORE! Now you will know the horror, Freeza!" Goku surrounds himself with golden energy, flies toward Freeza, punches him in the face, breaks his back across his knee, and while still in mid-air hits Freeza with a double axe handle that sends him crashing into the ground, forming a massive crater and dust cloud. Goku takes his first step on the long road of vengeance.

What follows is one of the most epic and drawn out fights in anime history. Too long to describe in words. At the end of the bloody day, Goku is the victor and Freeza is so defeated that he begs for mercy.

Goku, despite being a Super Saiya-jin powered by narrow minded rage, still has kindness in his heart and gives Freeza the mercy he doesn't deserve. "You've been defeated," he says, "Now stop fighting and change your evil ways." Goku gives Freeza some of his *ki*, powers down from Super Saiya-jin, and flies away.

Freeza then uses Goku's very compassion against him, firing a single *ki* blast while he had his back turned. This was a foolish mistake caused by his unwillingness to change, a stubborn refusal to see the truth of his reality, and a proud, boastful, elitist attitude that made him blind to his own condition. Goku gives him a chance at redemption and he throws it away.

Goku is unable to see an alternative and is forced to do what he never wants to do.

Kill.

2.5.6 History Repeats Itself

Both history and the stories we tell of it are about depicting human behavior through time, and the storytelling pattern in "It's over 9,000!" repeats itself for as long as Scouter technology continues to be used. There's always a unique twist, but really it's the same old thing each time. An alien uses the Scouter to judge someone, they underestimate their opponent by putting them into a labeled box, the opponent is a spiritual warrior and should not be underestimated, and then they power up and defeat the alien.

For some strange reason after that *incredibly climactic event* in which Freeza's death is *confirmed* by North Kaiō and Planet Namek explodes, Akira Toriyama decides to keep Freeza alive anyway, and this conflict of worldviews continues with the newly revived and robotically enhanced "Mecha" Freeza and his newly introduced father, King Cold.

Father and son arrive on Earth to seek revenge against Goku. They land with their giant insect-like space ship and see a mysterious boy waiting for them. It's Trunks, *another* Super Saiya-jin who traveled back in time and is trained in the same power controlling method as the others.

Huh? Well that was unexpected. Especially for Vegeta, since his nemesis is not only still alive, but there's now a *second* Super Saiya-jin.

Even though Trunks kills several of Freeza's men in a split second and it should be obvious that he is strong, King Cold follows the now cliché pattern of using the Scouter to read his power level, and it says "5." Freeza tells his father not to pay attention to the number, because these earthlings can control their power output. Despite knowing this from bitter, firsthand experience, both Freeza and his father end up repeating the same old mistake and being killed by Trunks. All before Goku even makes it back home from his outer space adventures.

Why did they repeat the same mistake? Because their worldview was still the same. Freeza didn't change, he just had the Super Saiya-jin awaken, issue a beat down, and almost kill him. Now for most people that would probably be cause for self reflection, but not for Freeza. He managed to survive and had a chance to look within, but he held on to his elitist notions and his vision became even *more* narrow. That's why he was on

Earth after all, to seek revenge. As a result, both he and his father lost their lives.

What's continually fascinating about this dynamic is that it never feels played out, and you don't even realize it's repeating itself because the stakes keep getting higher. You're so shocked by this mysterious youth with golden hair that you don't even stop to think about the things described in this book. That's because what the viewer sees in the series is the multifaceted conflict that occurs when worldviews collide. The storytelling and character development is engaging and believable each and every time.

2.6 Vegeta is Multifaceted

The characters in *Dragon Ball* are not black and white, but Scouters make it seem that one person is "better" and the other person "worse." It simplifies people and equates their value with a number. It puts others into classes and makes the Scouter users' world a little easier to move around in because they can identify themselves by labeling others. Unfortunately, that mentality is not beneficial for anyone.

The characters in *Dragon Ball* are multifaceted and there are no "bad guys" or "good guys" beyond the roles they play in the story. Just like the rest of us, each person can be viewed from multiple angles and when analyzing a seemingly bad guy such as Vegeta, the more you look at the world from his point of view the more sympathy and understanding you have for his violent behavior. In short, he was a product of his genetics, but even more so his environment.

In an interview with *ComicBookResources.com* on April 2, 2009, James Marsters, the actor who played Piccolo in the 20th Century Fox live-action Hollywood adaptation called *Dragonball Evolution*, answered a question about how he perceives the clashing worldviews in the *Dragon Ball* series. James said, "In Shakespeare, there are really no villains or heroes, there'd just be people behaving in a villainous manner or a heroic manner, and it depends on which chapter of their life you happen to climb in on as to where they fit in the story. And I think that *Dragon Ball* has the same kind of universe where people start really evil and get redeemed in a fairly realistic way. Not like they're all butter and cookies all of a sudden, but they do switch sides and they do realize certain things. I think that takes it away from white hats and black hats stapled on characters, which is less interesting."

The most interesting thing about Vegeta isn't that he grows up in a repressive society built on class struggle and manages to break past it through his own efforts, but that he purposefully projects the repressive society mentality he grew up with onto others. It's like when a parent beats a child and the child grows up and has their own kids and beats them too. The negative behavior passes onto others.

For example, King Vegeta instilled in Vegeta's mind that he was better than others, so when fighting Goku he repeatedly talks about how Goku is a "low class" warrior from a "low class" father. He pushes Goku down and builds himself up. But Goku turns that judgment on its' head and says he's thankful for it because it allowed him to come to Earth and meet all of his friends. The box can't hold him.

When that strategy of self validation stops working, then Vegeta talks about how he is superior to Freeza's men because he no longer needs the Scouter. That sort of backfires and he almost dies fighting Zarbon. So while continuing to say that he is superior he also talks about how he is the Legendary Super Saiya-jin incarnate, and will be the death of all his opponents. This doesn't come to fruition either, and Goku one ups him again by beating him to that level.

After this he resorts to his all-purpose fallback by calling himself "The Prince of all Saiya-jins," because surely no one can take that away from him. Despite the fact that according to the canon storyline, Goku is the only full blooded Saiya-jin left in the universe. So is he saying he's Goku's prince? No, not really. It's a proud, boastful statement, an emotional recognition of who he is and where he came from. Even after coming to Earth he still thinks more highly of himself than others.

The root of Vegeta's self-validating statements is a denial of an internal weakness in his character. He makes these external proclamations as a crutch to hold up his own fragile ego in the face of someone better. He holds onto it for as long as he can until it stops working, and then moves onto the next crutch a little bit deeper in his psyche and personal identity.

Vegeta comes from a privileged background and feels he has to uphold that. His identity is centered on the pride that because he was born with these inherent abilities he *should* be better than everyone else. That's the whole source of his identity. Without that, he's nothing. It's actually very fragile and yet this pride is the origin of his power and motivation to constantly be the best. He simply *must* be stronger than Goku. He simply *must* be stronger than Freeza. He simply *must* be stronger than the Artificial Humans. He simply *must* be stronger than Cell, and so on.

Why does Vegeta do this? Because it protects him from facing the truth of his own unhappy, painful life. The fact his father is dead. His partner is dead. His entire race is dead and the only one left is a foolish clown. On top of that he spent the first 30 years of his life unwillingly serving a maniacal despot. It's no wonder he looks so angry!

Vegeta wants happiness just like every man does, and he finds happiness in being the best. But all of his victories and triumphs are short lived because Goku always manages to go one step higher or an opponent appears out of nowhere with more power. His life is poetically bittersweet. Filled with hardship and short lived glory of momentous heights, all in an effort to avoid anguish and find happiness. As a result, Vegeta projects his unhappiness onto others in order to avoid dealing with the pain. In the meantime he chases external goals, always seeking to be better than others and never really achieving the long term validation or self satisfaction he desires.

In comparison to his rival, Goku's genetic father was also killed by Freeza, but Goku was ignorant of that knowledge until he was already an adult, and he, unlike Vegeta, had a positive outlook and nurturing role models from the beginning. Goku later unknowingly killed his own adoptive father, Son Gohan, as a transformed Ōzaru, and also spent his remaining teenage years fatherless. But he felt no bitterness and continued to live his life alone in the mountains. He was a happy go lucky country boy without a care in the world (except his next meal). Goku was then raised by one martial arts master after another who treated him with kindness and taught lessons of positivity, tolerance and optimism. He had many father figures who cared for him deeply.

Human beings are meant to grow in a positive and accepting environment but Vegeta's worldview is grounded on a negative and dismissive environment. Such an environment is not conducive to tapping into hidden potential. It leads to constraint, frustration, bitterness and selfishness. That's why Vegeta learned to rely on himself and be consistently derisive of others. So much so that as a child Vegeta had already become heartless and dead inside, not only by slaughtering thousands of innocent people across the galaxy, but by his complete indifference to the elimination of his own race.

Both Goku and Vegeta share a strong work ethic, and are constantly pushing themselves, but Goku ends up being stronger than Vegeta in the end. It's because Goku's worldview is built on a positive environment and Vegeta's is built on a negative environment. Even so, Vegeta is remarkable because despite growing up in that horribly violent, narcissistic environment that shapes his entire worldview, he manages to enlighten to the reality that his life is not fixed. He can change the situation if he can only find a way.

For Vegeta, his way of change is pride, and it becomes the source of all his strength. It's pride that keeps him motivated, pride that keeps him rising up to the next level, and pride that allows him to survive as long as he does. There is an iconic scene in the FUNimation dub that is now synonymous with Vegeta's character. It occurs after he willingly allows himself to become possessed by the wicked sorcerer Babidi in exchange for more power. Power that he desired so he could defeat Goku. Vegeta now resists Babidi's mind control efforts in order to regain control, and he screams, "You can take control of my mind and body, but there is one thing a Saiyan always keeps... his PRIDE!" He erupts in an explosion of golden light, the evil spirits pour out of his body and he regains control of his mind, with all the newly tapped power still in place. Vegeta *is* his pride.

It's only at the very end of *Dragon Ball Z* after a long process of character development and personal change where Vegeta finally, *finally* admits that Goku is better than he is. It's Vegeta's last shining moment: The glorious culmination of his role as an anti-hero, as Goku's ally, as a lover and father, and as a reluctant savior of the universe.

He lets go of his attachments and gives Goku a thumbs up!

2.6.1 BLUE, RED, AND GOLD

Goku and Vegeta are rivals because of their difference in perspectives caused by the environment in which they were raised. But at their core they share a mindset that no one else in the cosmos can understand, for they are the last two full blooded Saiya-jins alive. Their similarities ensure their fates are tied together and they help one another develop like the interwoven *yīn* and *yáng* in a *tàijí*.

I interviewed Ryō Horikawa, the Japanese voice actor of Vegeta at Anime Expo 2012 in Los Angeles, California. I asked him his thoughts on the rivalry between Goku and Vegeta, and whether or not he felt *Dragon Ball* was a meaningful series. Ryō said, "I think Dragon Ball is something like the Bible. It has a really important philosophy to it. As far as the rivalry goes, they are sometimes rivals and they also sometimes work together to fight other enemies. I think that helps the story."

Vegeta needs Goku and Goku needs Vegeta because opposites attract and have a mutually beneficial relationship. The *tàijí* that is commonly understood consists of black and white *qì* (or *ki*), but that's actually a low level Dao. The higher level Great Primordial Dao talked about in ancient scriptures consists of a blue and red higher energy. Vegeta is blue. Goku is red. One leads, the other follows, and then their roles reverse. They continuously rotate up to higher levels by following the traditional *shugyō* self-cultivation method inherent in East Asian cultural belief systems, where similar events continue occurring at increasingly higher levels with the purpose of refining the practitioner.

Over time their worlds meld together and Goku becomes more like Vegeta while Vegeta becomes more like Goku. Vegeta learns to look within, starts a family on Earth and overcomes his ego (to a degree). Goku learns to accept his Saiya-jin roots, attain Super Saiya-jin and control his primal power to the point where he is calm yet strong. Vegeta chases Goku the entire time, but he walks his own path while doing it. Later in the series Goku and Vegeta literally fuse together and become a new sentient being that is neither Vegeta nor Goku, known as Vegetto (the Japanese pronunciation of their Saiya-jin names, Vegeta and Kakarotto combined)!

They fight one another because that's the most direct path to change. To quote another seminal martial arts epic, in *The Matrix Reloaded* (2003), the Oracle's guardian called Seraph finishes testing Neo in combat and says to him, "I had to know if you were the One." Neo responds with a smirk, "You could have just asked." Seraph says, "No. You do not truly know someone until you fight them." And so it is with Vegeta and Goku. They fight one another to better understand themselves and increase their power level. They're Saiya-jins after all, so their first priority is their own personal development, but by learning about themselves they also learn about others.

Dragon Ball is all about reaching higher and higher levels. This is because *Journey to the West* is filled with Buddho-Daoist symbolism and mythos of supernormal powers, and it is the inspirational source material of *Dragon Ball*. In self-cultivation, practitioners are primarily concerned with the issue of levels. The cosmic structure and hierarchy of the Buddho-Daoist worldview involves multiple realms and dimensions of increasingly high levels. That is to say, levels on top of levels, with unique realms of space-time, such as when they refer to "9 levels of Heaven" or "81 levels of Heaven." The more they improve themselves, the higher their level rises. With that ascension arrives new abilities and a broader enlightenment. It's the same story in *Dragon Ball*, particularly when you look at Goku.

Recall their first fight on Earth. Vegeta thought he knew everything about Goku–'He's low level trash and the scum of Saiya-jin society.' 'It's an honor for this clown to even be fighting and subsequently killed by a super elite.'–But no, that turns out to not be the case. Goku and his friends defeat Vegeta and not only that, Goku spares his life, allowing him to escape in his Saiya-jin space pod. From that moment onward Vegeta has a lot of learning to do. Beginning with a newfound understanding of *ki*, of men and their potential. Vegeta starts to *feel*. Vegeta takes the Scouter off and chooses to no longer look at the world through its lens. Symbolically to no longer be like the rest of the aliens. Vegeta goes through such a fundamental transformation that in the face of death he even cries and asks Goku for help. He faces up to the unobstructed truth of his own life. He understands for the first time that life is not determined by what family you're born into or what others try to force upon you. Instead, life is what you make of it!

Goku fulfills the role that Vegeta always strove for simply by being Goku. He didn't even know about the Super Saiya-jin Legend and doesn't fit the description, and yet he's the one who attains it, defeats Freeza and redeems all of the fallen Saiya-jin people. He isn't attached, he doesn't need to validate himself, and yet he gets their naturally without pursuit. Goku already knew what Vegeta still had to enlighten to. He was way ahead of the game and had gone far beyond. He just wasn't as technically powerful when they first met because he didn't have strong enough opponents to push him to that level.

When Goku or Vegeta hit a wall in their training, they both look for a way past it. But the fundamental difference between Goku and Vegeta is that Goku doesn't look externally. He's not chasing someone else. In Buddhism it's said that looking externally for solutions leads to a demonic path, just like when Vegeta allows himself to be possessed and become a *Majin* in order to increase his power. Goku is not inherently Buddhist and doesn't ascribe to any religious beliefs, but his character and the *Dragon Ball* universe are rooted in that belief system. Goku always looks *inside* for the answers and is able to perpetually ascend higher and higher up the ladder of self-development on his own merits.

It's said in Buddhist scriptures that when a being has the desire to cultivate, it "Shines like gold and shakes the world of ten directions." That statement refers to a being's "Buddha Nature" coming forth and creating shock waves in the spherical ten directional worldview of the universe, expanding outwardly through the macroscopic cosmos and contracting inwardly through the microscopic atoms. It can also be seen as an analogy of the moment of enlightenment, or specifically of the concept of "sudden enlightenment," referred to in Japanese *zen* Buddhism as *satori* (悟り). The first character in *satori* (悟) is the same as in Goku's name (悟空) and means enlightened, aware, or awakened. There's no one that can keep Goku down because he makes the choice to allow himself to be free. Every hardship is another step on the cultivation path, and that is why he is the first to ascend.

Goku teaches Vegeta what it truly means to go "Over 9,000!" It means to work so damn hard that you break the bonds of "destiny," you burst the box of labels, you force others to say, "There's no way that can be right, can it?" You become so good they can't ignore you!

To do this requires self-confidence, honesty, kindness and endurance. It also requires letting go of incorrect or inhibiting notions. It's about defeating ones' false self in order for the true self to be born. When the lies that obstruct the mind are removed, the true self ascends to the surface. When it finally breaks free, it shines like gold.

2.6.2 VEGETA AWAKENS!

To see these concepts in action, let's take a look at *Dragon Ball Z* episode 129, titled "The Might of Vegeta, The Blood of a Super Saiya-jin Awakens." As you can imagine, it is in this episode that Vegeta finally attains his desires.

Vegeta is on Earth fighting against Artificial Human 19 and Artificial Human 20. In the American English dub by FUNimation he delivers a monologue about his newly displayed, shocking power.

> **Vegeta:** "My motivation was very different than Kakarot's. My motivation was to be the *best*. To be the greatest Saiyan alive, as I always had been, until Kakarot came into the picture, that is."
>
> *Vegeta recalls his training in pursuit of overcoming Goku.*
>
> **Vegeta:** "Kakarot's success was like a demon in my head. How could *he* be a Super Saiyan, when *I*, the prince of *all* Saiyans, could not? The intensity of my training was *maddening*. At 450 times normal gravity, a basic training game became a desperate struggle for survival. Even the simplest moves required every ounce of willpower I had. I wasn't sure how long I could sustain the effort without breaking in two. It seemed like the only thing holding my body together was my *one* desire: To be *better* than Kakarot! At times I thought I was *losing my mind*. Why couldn't I obtain what Kakarot had obtained? It didn't make sense. It was infuriating! And it was my *fury* that kept me alive."

Vegeta continues telling his story.

Vegeta: "I decided to continue my training in the solitude of space where I would be unhindered by the distractions of the Earth. And when a violent electrical storm erupted in the skies of the planet I was on, I welcomed it. It seemed fitting, like it was an outward manifestation of the storm that was *raging inside of me!*"

A nearby asteroid breaks apart due to the catastrophic planetary storm.

Vegeta: "Then the meteors started coming down, but I was determined to survive and to protect my ship from destruction. It was my *only* way out, my *only* way off that nightmarish heap of rubble. I thought I had everything under control, but then the mother of all meteors seemed to *appear out of nowhere* to claim my ship, and my life. Normally it would have been child's play to blow up that rock, but after training in 450 times normal gravity for so long, it took everything I had, and more!"

Vegeta fires a ki blast at the meteor with such power that it causes a part of it to explode, blasting him downward into the planet's surface as the rest of the meteor continues approaching. A moment later Vegeta emerges from the dust, covered in blood. He screams.

Vegeta: "Kakarot!"

The story returns to Vegeta on Earth as he recalls the moment.

Vegeta: "Then something just *snapped*, something *inside* of me."

The story goes back to the planet.

Vegeta: "No. NO MORE! That's it! I don't CARE!"

Vegeta pounds his bloody fist on the ground. His body quakes with anger.

He continues to narrate on Earth as the deadly events unfold on the planet.

Vegeta: "I didn't *care* anymore. I didn't *care* about being better than Kakarot. I didn't *care* about being a Super Saiyan. I didn't *care* if I *lived*. I didn't *care* about *anything*!

A trigger goes off in Vegeta's mind.

Vegeta: "And then, it happened."

His eyes open wide and he starts screaming as golden light begins to emanate from his body.

Vegeta: "AAAAAAAGHHHHHHHHHHHHHH!!!"

Vegeta becomes a Super Saiyan as omnidirectional rays of golden light burst out of his body and into outer space.

This is the *end* of Vegeta's journey that *started* with his encounter with Goku during the "It's over 9,000!" scene. It's the point where Vegeta lets go of his attachment, his worldview of being a "super elite," and stops chasing Goku. Why? Because he had no other choice! Alone on a planet about to be destroyed by an impending meteor (literally between a rock and a hard place), Vegeta stops caring, lets go of his desires and concerns for self validation, and even the attachment to life and death. This is the precise moment where "something inside" of him "snaps."

Vegeta's survival is only possible because his mind changes so dramatically in the face of impending destruction. He goes from a narrow minded, externally driven worldview, to a broad minded, internally empty worldview. In the right conditions, at the right time, he travels from one polar extreme to the other and this causes him to transform.

Why didn't Vegeta attain Super Saiya-jin earlier despite his training being even more intense than Goku's on his way to Planet Namek? Because despite all the changes Vegeta goes through and all the suffering he endures, he still doesn't have the right worldview. He is still too narrowly focused on being better than someone else.

It's only when he poetically *loses* that worldview that he *gains* sudden enlightenment (*satori*). A trigger goes off in his mind, the higher level energy (that was already present deep inside his sub-consciousness) is unlocked as the microcosmic gates in his body burst open, and golden beams of light spread out in "10 directions" as the planet shakes.

Vegeta awakens!

Vegeta finally attains Super Saiya-jin and becomes the best, and he does it in the opposite manner of Goku. Goku followed Vegeta's dying wish and became less naïve. With the imminent threat of Freeza's power, Goku was forced to go from broad to narrow and snap via anger because of the loss of his friends. Vegeta is dead on the inside and has no friends (except for his own ego), so how does he transform? It's the external environment of fatal activity that forces him to let go of that perspective. He's alone on a cold, dead planet in the middle of an electrical storm with a gigantic meteor coming to kill him, and he's *fighting against himself*. There's no external enemy to direct his anger toward. It's just him and the rock. In this scenario he is forced to let go of his narrow minded vision, stop caring completely about his pursuits, go broad and become the polar opposite of his normal self.

For the two full blooded Saiya-jins to enlighten and tap into their full potential and survive, they had to adopt the other's worldview for a brief moment in time.

2.6.3 "It's Over 9,000!" Points to our own Humanity

What do two earthlings and aliens killing one another in *Dragon Ball Z* have to do with you? When you started this book you probably never considered the question, but as it turns out, the answer is "a lot," because "It's over 9,000!" and Goku and Vegeta's life stories can show you what it means to be a better human.

The best stories are the ones that speak to our humanity. *Dragon Ball* is special because not only does it relate to what each of us goes through in life, it awakens a subtle part that yearns to be better than we currently are. It makes us believe in the power of change.

"It's over 9,000!" and the story behind Vegeta and Goku's worldviews reveals an important lesson. When people want to exceed their current level, there will be obstructions that oppose them. Where there is *yīn* there is *yáng*. Almost every main character in the series wants to be the most powerful and is unwilling to accept their limitations. The "good guys" and the "bad guys" are the same in this regard. Even Bulma, who has no fighting ability whatsoever, continues to work on her scientific inventions and push herself harder (while wicked scientists create killer robots in opposition to the heroes). And without Bulma the *Dragon Ball* story would never have begun. So no matter your gender, race, creed, location, intelligence or physical abilities, you have untapped potential that can be realized, no matter the obstacles that seem to inhibit progress. Obstructions are there to serve as guardians of the next threshold, to protect the gates of the limits that need to be broken through in your mind.

Dragon Ball was written for and aimed directly at a demographic of young fans. They see that the greater the challenge Goku, Vegeta, Gohan, Trunks and others face, the faster their improvement, and everything is possible when they commit to achieve it. *Dragon Ball* uses action and fighting to teach you that you *can* reach your full potential. All it takes is learning to look within and the endurance to work hard. If you can be honest with yourself, merciful to others, and endure, then you can succeed.

As children we grow up wanting to be heroes. Or in the case of Vegeta, an anti-hero with enormous confidence and pride. Why? Because heroes (and anti-heroes) defeat opponents and overcome challenges that normal people cannot. They climb the tallest mountains, strike down the scariest monsters and complete the impossible tasks. It's like a fairy tale or Greek myth come to life. The wild wishes of youth seem all too achievable with just the right type of training and the consistent will to apply it.

This is appealing because there is an inherent desire in all of us to exceed our limitations. Every person has it, but some of us are so covered up with notions, desires, concepts, fears and socially enforced garbage that we can no longer see the spark within our soul. As kids we're taught we can do anything and become anyone if we dream big, work hard enough and tap into our potential. But as we age, our time, abilities and dreams become more limited. Our minds become more narrow minded and we get lost, just like the aliens who are always looking externally, chasing after the dragon balls to satisfy their desires or comfort their fears. They pursue one thing after another and yet they never find what they are looking for because they don't look within.

Ask yourself, 'When is it too late to become who I really want to be?' In your teens, in your 20s or 30s? *Dragon Ball* teaches that it's NEVER too late to change. Vegeta was 29 years old when he arrived on Earth and fought Goku. He continued to change for the rest of his life.

The noteworthy factor in Goku's life is that he didn't start out special. He was considered trash; so low his father didn't want to acknowledge his existence. Goku didn't have a rich education, a wealthy upbringing or any friends in power to open back doors. Every single thing that Goku earned in life, he earned himself through hard work, dedication, and following his masters' disciplined requirements at each level.

Vegeta on the other hand, had it all. He was born a "super elite," the son of King Vegeta, the strongest of all Saiya-jins. Endowed with wealth, power, and raised to be a ruthless warrior, Vegeta thrived on proving his superiority. He was subservient to Lord Freeza out of necessity, but in his heart he still believed himself the better man. Vegeta had intelligence, strength, and the strongest pride of any character in the history of anime, yet it was Goku who defeat him! Vegeta then spends the remaining years of his life attempting to become more powerful than Goku and enact his revenge. With every passing day and each new opponent he taps into more of his incredible potential, but it is only when he finally lets go of that pursuit that he ascends.

It is important to remember that both Goku and Vegeta are full blooded Saiya-jins, and their number one focus in life is reaching the next level of their training. That's a big part of their personalities and the message of the series as a whole. Figure out what is important to you and focus on achieving it. So it would be wrong to say that Vegeta becomes a super hero of some sort or becomes just like Goku after his ascension. No, he's still Vegeta after all, and the mindset that triggered his sudden enlightenment was only temporary. His rivalry with Goku picks right back up after he realizes how powerful he has become (validating his existence), and especially so when Goku somehow becomes *even stronger*. And it's the same with Goku, who is still a care free and happy guy most of the time. Their extreme changes in worldview are necessary and temporary manifestations of a will to survive in extreme situations.

This obsessive mentality with reaching the next level often causes problems with family, in the same way that a modern day workaholic can ignore or alienate family members that want their attention. For example, Goku, despite being pure hearted and incredible in many ways, is also an absentee father figure for years at a time. He's either dead or training somewhere else in the world other than at home near his wife, Chi-Chi. In contrast, Vegeta is arguably a decent father once you get past his external toughness and seeming lack of sentimentality. He never shows any outward affection or even holds his son as he's growing up. He also purposefully punches him in the face while training. (Tough love?) But he *does* care for his son and eventual daughter, and for Bulma, although they never marry. Despite only knowing his father for a few years before his death, and his horrible upbringing under Freeza where he learns to be a cold hearted murderer, Vegeta turns out to be an okay dad. He spends time with his kids and is usually at the Capsule Corporation headquarters with Bulma. And he later makes the ultimate sacrifice in order to protect his family: He gives up his life so that *they* can continue to live. It could be said that in some ways he's an even better father than Goku, which is ironic given the huge difference in their worldviews when they first met. The way Vegeta transforms into a family man on Earth and the way his family changes him and becomes his new source of motivation, is perhaps the greatest testament of Vegeta's personal development.

Goku on the other hand sees everybody with the same merciful, compassionate mindset, in a rather unattached, universal love kind of manner. (Or he's just absent minded and doesn't care, depending on your perspective). Recall that he doesn't play favorites, and saves Dende and Mister Satan instead of his own sons and Vegeta's son when the time arrives for him to choose while fighting Majin Buu. For the most part Goku is not swayed by his familial attachments. His motivation is to be strong enough to save others, and that's why he's often considered a messianic figure. So much so that a "Church of Goku" has sprung up in Spain and other Spanish speaking countries, where they view Goku as their moral role model. That's the impact *Dragon Ball* has on their lives.

2.6.4 DRAGON BALL INSPIRES

One of the many reasons why *Dragon Ball* has such a huge fan base is that it inspires. The actions of Goku, Vegeta and the other main characters inspire us to take actions and be more like them. It's a huge part of the *Dragon Ball* fandom. Fans see them "powering up" and *they* want to get powered up. Especially for boys who want to get super huge muscles in the gym or train in the martial arts. But it's not only limited to physical change, or boys for that matter.

On *The Dao of Dragon Ball Blog*, a fan named Monica shared her story of how Vegeta gave her more confidence. Monica said, "I like the tenacity of his character and I identify with him a lot. My favorite thing about Vegeta is that he's not always the best, but he's always trying to be. Vegeta gets kind of a bad reputation, but sometimes charging in guns blazing is the best way to do things, especially if over thinking it is your weakness." A few months after the interview she got a tattoo of the Saiya-jin royal crest on her wrist. She said, "The truth is, I have anger issues mostly due to anxiety and frustration at wanting to accomplish more. I have a tendency to get angry and yell at people or confront them, but all my anger comes from lack of confidence. So yes, I do identify with Vegeta and I relate to his flaws, but I also try to learn from his confidence. I feel like the tattoo will remind me to be more confident." For Monica, *Dragon Ball* is more than just action and fights, it's about connecting with the characters and story. "The reason Vegeta is my favorite is because I think he has the best character development. He's the one that drew me into it." The Saiya-jin royal crest is a symbol of pride for Vegeta, and for Monica her tattoo serves as a reminder to value her own self worth.

A young man named Joshua also shared his story on *The Dao of Dragon Ball Blog*, saying that he relied on Goku's worldview to help him persevere through a dark valley of life. In 2011, Joshua recently lost his job and had to move back in with his parents. He said, "I was not in a good place.

I didn't want to talk to anyone, see anyone, or have anything to do with anything. I had no social life and just sat in my room and stared at the ceiling." Things were not going well and he was depressed and alone. This led to thoughts of suicide.

Fortunately he had *Dragon Ball*. "An idea came out of me being at the lowest point in my life. I said, 'I want to rewatch all of *Dragon Ball*, *Dragon Ball Z*, and *Dragon Ball GT*, straight through in its' canonical order.'" Watching the entire series from beginning to end is a significant challenge because there are 508 episodes, but Joshua felt it was something he had always wanted to do and decided that if he was going to die soon, then he might as well give it a try. "I just thought, 'I'm going to watch *Dragon Ball*, and then I'm probably going to kill myself.' That was the idea. 'I'm going to watch it one last time and then take some pills.'"

Joshua planned to record his journey on a blog so he could stay on track. He said, "I start watching them and doing the blog, and almost immediately I begin feeling better because I'm watching *Dragon Ball*. From the first time *Makafushigi Adventure* comes on I'm like, 'Aw yeah, I'm happy again.'" *Makafushigi Adventure* (English: Mystical Adventure) is the introduction theme song to the original *Dragon Ball*, and its' positive and light hearted spirit caused him to change. "It was one of those things where I was depressed but there was still a part of my brain that said, 'You CAN get through this. Set yourself a goal and at the end of the goal reevaluate your situation.'"

As Joshua continued watching the episodes his outlook improved rapidly. "The more I watched *Dragon Ball* the more I felt that this is the most incredible show I've ever seen." He had been a fan for years, but now the message of personal change was reaching him loud and clear. He said, "*Dragon Ball* is such an integral part of who I am and such a big thing I love that it's always going to make me feel better. Goku and the other characters around him influence me in a positive way. I can improve!" Joshua had always felt a special connection with Goku and he admired Goku's optimistic worldview of personal change. "Goku was my moral barometer from age 11 onward. He's pure. He's an ideal. Now when I'm in a spot where I'm not sure what to do, I think, 'What would Goku do here?' And I move past it that way."

Joshua's story makes it clear that *Dragon Ball* changes lives. He changed from a depressed young man trapped in his own mind, to a positive, outgoing blogger connecting with *Dragon Ball* fans across the world who appreciate and support him. He started his *Dragon Ball* blog for what he called, "self medication." Watching Goku on his adventures gave him the inspiring, uplifting medicine he needed to pull through. He said, "*Dragon Ball* is a feel-good show. Even at its darkest there is always an emotional pay off if you keep enduring. Really so much about it is thinking positive. As ridiculous and simple as it sounds, if you think positive you'll feel positive." Without *Dragon Ball* Joshua may no longer be here, and because he adopted Goku's worldview he survived the dark valley and gained greater insight. Like his moral role model, Joshua was able to endure the pain and keep going. That's the secret of Goku's success, and Joshua's too.

The alien worldview in *Dragon Ball* suggests that people are fixed at birth and cannot change, but the *Dragon Ball* story confirms the mindset of personal change is real and reminds us of it if we have forgotten. It inspires us to look within, mature, and be determined to reach the next level. Now when Monica is frustrated she looks at her tattoo and thinks of what Vegeta had to overcome, and when Joshua is suffering he asks, 'What would Goku do?'

Whether it's striving to be more confident like Vegeta, live with positive values like Goku, or improve your character in another way, *Dragon Ball* teaches that if you have the insight to imagine that it's possible and the wisdom to put it into action, then you can reach your full potential. Think about how many mental and physical challenges Goku and Vegeta endure. In the end they both know it's really this simple: Suffer the pain of discipline or suffer the pain of regret. At the end of the day they have a smile on their face because they live according to their values and go the distance.

The message in *Dragon Ball* is hopeful and resonates with every human being. No matter who you are or where you come from, you *can* tap into your potential and attain "Over 9,000!" And with enough hard work you can become your own version of a Super Saiya-jin.

2.7 THE 3 BIG TAKEAWAYS

Here are the 3 big takeaways of *Dragon Ball* present in the "It's over 9,000!" scene.

1. There is growth through conflict because when worldviews collide it forces one to change.

2. Extreme opposites attract and provide the best cultivation scenario to improve.

3. There is no gain without loss. In order to be free, a person has to let go of their previous habits, concepts and notions, in spite of difficult external factors. When they do, they will ascend!

In Part 3 you'll learn how "It's over 9,000!" is a perfect microcosmic slice of the greater macrocosmic story of *Dragon Ball* and why it became so popular across the world.

PART 3

A Thin Slice of
Dragon Ball

In Part 1 you learned what "It's over 9,000!" was all about. In Part 2 you discovered the significance of this scene as it relates to the human condition. Now in Part 3 you'll learn how "It's over 9,000!" is an example of a meme that represents a small slice of the bigger *Dragon Ball* story, a simple video, image, joke, and phrase that has all the necessary ingredients to shed light on the underlying themes prevalent in the series as a whole. You'll see that "It's over 9,000!" represents a single letter in the evolving pop cultural language that is the *Dragon Ball* alphabet. The impact "It's over 9,000!" had in the *Dragon Ball* community and Internet community is still felt today.

The main reason "It's over 9,000!" became popular was because of an existing *Dragon Ball* community that is large and global. *Oricon* is a Japanese company that monitors and reports on the sales of entertainment media. On August 7, 2012, *Oricon* released a global report that showed *Dragon Ball* as the world's most recognized anime and manga among the general public, not just anime fans. The "Over 9,000!" phenomenon was only able to flourish because a community already existed that had the knowledge to understand its meaning and transform it into a meme. In other words it wouldn't have gone viral unless there were people out there who "got it." Without those people who shared the clip with others it would have simply been one of the other countless funny videos that hits the Internet and falls flat.

Dragon Ball is filled with rich history, eastern influences, pop cultural references, fairy tales, legends and beliefs that continue to inspire generations of children and young adults today. It is but one of many spin-off phenomena within the larger *Dragon Ball* phenomenon that has occurred over the years such as the most recent "Super Saiyan's are Real" video. So what made "It's over 9,000!" so successful?

Thanks to the Internet there is now a reactive relationship between content creators and content consumers. It's no longer a 1-to-many relationship as has been the case in previous decades and media. It's now a 1-to-many-to-community cycle. That means one person creates something and it reaches other people, who then repurpose or alter it slightly while adding their own personal stamp and then share it with others again. This is the nature of an Internet meme and likewise the nature of a subculture focused community like the one *Dragon Ball* fans belong to. When you have both, the meme spreads like wildfire, evolves rapidly, and is able to reach outside the subculture.

Memes are created and spread all the time because people want to share humorous things. *Dragon Ball* is targeted towards adolescents, a group of individuals who are trying to figure out who they are. The perfect age group: Young enough to have an imagination and belief that everything is still possible, yet old enough to start navigating the world, seek direction, find role models, and make connections. Some connect to Krillin (the average Joe), Vegeta (the alpha male), or Goku (the hero). Everybody has a character they can relate to. So it becomes a cool thing to say "It's Over 9,000!" and have other people get it! This common ground makes discourse possible and the term thereby becomes popular because this fan base keeps it alive and makes it richer through humor.

Widening the scope further we see that the creation of *Dragon Ball* by Akira Toriyama, as well as his manga editors, the animation staff, musicians, producers, and everyone else involved, was given to the Japanese public and then the world community. The individuals within that world community then gave back to *Dragon Ball*, which reciprocated and gave back to the community again. The huge fan base spread the original *Dragon Ball* message, kept it alive and relevant so that decades after the original episode aired on Japanese TV, Kajetokun was able to rewatch, reuse, and repurpose the scene and people would *still* "get it." The meme's message and virality was only possible because of the globally connected community that both engaged and supported it. This engagement with the community strengthens the message, and in many ways *becomes* the message. The medium *is* the message. Without that it would have just been another random video.

TRANSFORMATION THROUGH LANGUAGE

In order to stand out amongst the modern deluge of information, there must be a compelling story or interplay of symbolism involved. This seemingly simple pop cultural reference became infused with an evolving Internet language. Today "It's over 9,000!" is both a standalone meme and a new term in pop cultural vernacular that spread through its humorous, colorful and memorable expression.

"It's over 9,000!" is popular for reasons beyond simply being funny. There are a lot of funny videos on the Internet and they don't all coin new terminology or catch on. Like the entire *Dragon Ball* series itself, there's an indefinable, special quality to "It's over 9,000!" that remains memorable and continues to be referenced. In time the humorous video, images and spin off jokes become nostalgic or gain more value. The larger the meme grows, the more it is used and starts to become cliché, meaning the meme could die at any moment. The reason "It's over 9,000!" has survived for so many years is because of the meaning applied by the fans who use it.

The modern age has become a society inundated with images, anime, music videos and other pop cultural references, creating a new kind of language: A system of symbols, a social media flow of information and emotional triggers. The advances in technology have greatly changed the context of communication. Because the context has changed, the content has changed along with it. In the case of *Dragon Ball*, what was once a static yet dynamic illustration on paper (the manga), is now a part of a fluid Internet culture, with a reflexive relationship between content creator and consumer.

As language continues to be an evolving vehicle of communication, it can manifest not only through words and images, but through rich storytelling. Languages constantly adapt to the changing external environment, and new words arise out of need, convenience or identity. In the modern age, a culture created via the current generation of technically savvy users now have a digital web of communication as their primary medium for dialogue, where a desktop computer, laptop, or mobile device becomes an extension of themselves. As a result, new words have been created to help communicate feelings or beliefs.

In ancient times the Greek *murios* and the Chinese *wàn* (both meaning 10,000 or "Over 10,000") served a similar purpose to "It's over 9,000!" when referring to large numbers. Over time the usage of *murios* fell out of favor in Western civilization and the modern age equivalent of "It's over 9,000!" seems to have arisen not only because of the popularity of *DBZ*, but because there was a genuine need to have a quantifiable term in the modern age. This need may possibly explain its widespread use and rampant popularity. People said "It's Over 9,000!" because the term was fun and useful in their everyday vocabulary.

Saying "Over 9,000!" is more symbolic and expressive today than saying "a lot." *Dragon Ball* has colored the common language of a generation and in so doing serves as a model of how to re-form language into something which becomes a more powerful vehicle of communication–A vehicle that is more suited to the current generation inundated with images and media, and who live a large portion of their life online.

SYMBOLS AND STORIES

The East Asian languages of Chinese and Japanese that *Dragon Ball* is derived from have an inherent characteristic at telling stories. Their written language, *kanji*, is an image based language, as *kanji* are illustrated images within images that contain meaning. An individual *kanji* can consist of other independent *kanji* that each denote their own meaning, and when combined denote a subtler connotation or greater meaning, creating the basis for language.

Manga is the natural evolution of this form of communication because it is a medium filled with illustrations. The illustrations themselves tell a story, but so do the words, written in *kanji*, *hiragana* and *katakana*. The action sound effects written across the page also tell a visual story as representations of sounds.

The profound importance of all this is that the images or phrases are devices used individually to tell a story and collectively to tell an even greater story. This holds enormous power as a form of communication. Whenever an image or concept tells a story it becomes a powerful language and vehicle of communication. When you combine this with animation and audio in the form of anime it becomes even more powerful. Adding interactivity, such as in the form of a video game causes a big impression on the one who experiences it, such as when FUNimation dubbed the lines again for *Dragon Ball Z: Burst Limit*. The collective story behind the manga, the anime, and the Internet meme as described in this book is all recollected by the player when playing the game, along with their expectation to watch the "It's over 9,000!" scene, and this causes the moment to be more engaging and memorable. In this sense the *Dragon Ball* world collides with our world through the meme.

Human beings have an innate longing to identify themselves within a community. Like many aspects of *Dragon Ball*, "It's over 9,000!" is just one example of how this pop cultural force became a part of an emerging language and urban slang. Aside from being useful it helps others identify with one another and connect. It pulls into our human need to communicate and belong; to be part of the in-joke or popular sayings. When "It's Over 9,000!" is spoken across the Internet by two people who understand it, they are immediately on common ground.

This book has shown that just like the written *kanji* characters of Japan, the symbolism and characteristics of "It's over 9,000!" can be dissected further down into smaller stories. The stories and meaning are what matter most, because these are what make the deepest impact on our language and thereby in ourselves.

MICRO AND MACRO

The microscopic lens I've shined on "It's over 9,000!" is purposeful, in what it says about the *Dragon Ball* series as a whole.

Although "It's over 9,000!" is a small segment, it contains all of the elements of *Dragon Ball Z*. The short clip has extremely muscular guys in martial arts uniforms, supernormal powers, spiky hair, screaming, explosions, references to ancient beliefs, futuristic technology, and underlying themes of the human condition.

"It's over 9,000!" subsequently became a new linguistic term that can be spoken, heard as audio, appear as an image, watched as video, worn as clothing, set up as action figures or played as a game. That is to say, this culture must be established for there to be genuine transformation in an individual, and it is through being influenced by this culture that an individual gains the ability to transform the culture back. Every time a new message is created and put on the Internet, or any other medium, it has the power to change lives. Even a message that seems simple or lacking in power can have a big effect when accepted, modified, and shared infinitum. "It's over 9,000!" is the perfect example of a simple message in the right context that was born from a culture and then changed that culture.

As a common part of the Millennial Generation's vernacular and Internet slang, "It's over 9,000!" affects people in subtle yet profound ways. One's language becomes part of their identity. To fully understand a culture you have to know its language, whether it's Chinese, Japanese, French, Italian, or "Internet," because without knowing the language you can't know the heart, spirit and culture of the people who speak it. For all of the people who say "It's Over 9,000!" on the Internet or in real life, their language, self-identity and social relationships have been altered. How much and in what ways depends on the individual.

Even so, it's fair to say that many people who clicked the "Like" button or shared it with their friends weren't hardcore *Dragon Ball* fans and certainly didn't think about it so deeply. Why then did it go viral? Because memes are symbolic of an evolving language shared by a community that *seeks to belong to itself.* The medium is the message and the message takes shape in the form of manga, anime, *YouTube* clips, and other formats and then shared with those within and without the community. Why? The same reason we all share things online, whether it's to laugh, bond, or recall fond memories.

Yet when something new is introduced into the *Dragon Ball* community that becomes viral it can alter the way people look at the series. Such as how Team Four Star's incredibly popular satirical videos on *YouTube* made Mister Popo seem creepy and weird. If you say the words "pecking order" to a *Dragon Ball* fan who is also a fan of those videos it means much more and is a lot funnier than saying, "a social hierarchy." The fans understand the characters so well that they can make in-jokes about other in-jokes, playing off the subtle relationship queues and odd moments. The language and the series itself become much richer replacements to the words that we normally use because now they're loaded with imagery, humor, and associations with the characters that fans have come to love.

The *Dragon Ball* series became not only a powerful storytelling medium, but one filled with messages and meaning that influenced the lives of many. "It's over 9,000!" serves the same purpose as the series but on a microscopic scale.

ONLY A THIN SLICE

In the same way that "It's over 9,000!" is a thin slice of the entire *Dragon Ball* series, this book is but a thin slice of what you will find in *The Dao of Dragon Ball* book series. This entire book was derived from about 1 minute of content from the series, but within this 1 minute there are so many meaningful insights that were revealed when examined fully.

The entire *Dragon Ball* series that Akira Toriyama draws upon to create his masterpiece is rich in centuries of history, culture, and the message of the human condition. He draws on all these elements and makes them his own unique creation.

In *The Dao of Dragon Ball* series I go into further detail about all of the underlying themes, including the martial arts cultures, religion, spirituality, character backgrounds, and conflicts in the series. I reveal the hidden elements, the complex interweaving of culture, history and storytelling, and in a sense decipher this code, this alphabet that is "*Dragon Ball*." Shedding light on how it becomes a very powerful new and influential pop cultural language. You will understand why the *Dragon Ball* series is the most popular anime and manga of all time. You'll find out where the Son Goku legend originates, how Goku compares to Superman, what the Japanese think of their own creation, how anger plays a role in the process of enlightenment, and so much more.

I will show you how profound stories can teach people and shape their lives to the point where it becomes the very reason they want to live. People resonate with *Dragon Ball* because it connects to the human spirit. If you're a lover of *Dragon Ball*, then you'll love to read the rest of *The Dao of Dragon Ball* series.

THE DRAGON SOUL WILL LIVE ON!

The original *Dragon Ball Z* episode featuring Vegeta screaming "It's over 8,000!" aired in 1991 in Japan, but the incorrectly dubbed English clip only became popular in 2006 because an American repurposed the content, modified it in a humorous way and distributed the video on a new global medium and platform. This made it more relevant to both existing and new audiences.

As long as the series gets enough exposure it will continually reach new generations. As *Dragon Ball* remains popular and relevant in people's lives, it's likely that new meaning will be further derived from the next generation of fans and another layer will be added on top of the storytelling onion.

Considering that *Dragon Ball* has been successful around the world and that fans continue to spend tens of millions of dollars each year on the franchise, *Dragon Ball* will live on. Even if the series is no longer officially supported, the love for *Dragon Ball* will always burn brightly in the hearts of fans because *Dragon Ball* appeals to our desire to go beyond limits, and the drive to be "Over 9,000!"

BRIAN DRUMMOND INTERVIEW

BRIAN DRUMMOND IS the voice actor behind, "It's Over 9,000!"

He is a Canadian voice actor famous for playing the roles of Vegeta in the Ocean dub of *Dragon Ball Z*, Zechs Merquise in *Mobile Suit Gundam Wing* (1995), Benny in *Black Lagoon* (2006), and Ryuk in *Death Note* (2006).

The content of this interview was recorded on May 20, 2015, during the making of my book, *Dragon Soul: 30 Years of Dragon Ball Fandom* (2015). This content is exclusive to the *"It's Over 9,000!"* book.

Q: When you recorded the "It's Over 9,000!" line you had no idea it would become a meme. How do you feel about this meme and the way people repeat your line just like you said it? It's your voice being heard by millions, and it stands for something. What does it mean to you?

There's something bizarre about the whole thing. The process of doing it was very mundane, and not something hugely pivotal in the series. It wasn't something pointed at by the director who said, 'Here's this point in the story, we really got to hit this, this is Oscar nomination time.' It was just another line on a day of screaming and doing our best at it. So to have someone put it together as a meme and have it take off as it did, is a bit bizarre.

On the day of recording, we tried to rewrite that line. I didn't want to say it because the word "thousand" didn't fit the length of the mouth flaps. This may be a case of it fitting in Japanese but not here, but whoever translated it didn't realize that it didn't fit by saying, "Over 9,000!"

When Nappa tells me about his power level, if I were going to yell that, my instinct as an actor is to be stunned and say, "What? Over 9,000!" at the pace of a normal person. Like, 'I can't believe that. How could he go from nothing to that amount, even though it's nowhere near my power level, how did that happen?' It's more about being stunned. So that's what I did, but it didn't fit.

My director, Karl Willems,[1] said, 'Brian, can you make that 'nine thousand' longer, because it's not fitting.' Okay, I say, "Over nine thousaaaaand." But that's still not long enough. Then I think, because his mouth stays open, let's change it to, "Nine thousand?! Noooo!" That way it's a bit more legit, instead of holding the word, "Nine thousaaaaaaaaaaaand." Who would do that? It's stupid, why would anybody do that? So I was fooling around with the line, but he says, 'Nah, it's not working, Brian.'

And the thing is, we only get paid by the line when dubbing in Canada, according to our union negotiations. We're paid by the line, so I don't want to sit on this line for a year. It's costing me money to not get lines done today. Let's get through 50 lines an hour, instead of one, and make some money. I just said, 'Fine, I'll really scream it as if he's flabbergasted by this, and you tell me how long it has to be.' So that's what I did: "IT'S OVER NINE THOUSAAAAAAAAAAAAND!!"

He said, 'Good, next line. Move on.' I thought it was ridiculous, and it didn't seem to fit. Then I completely forgot about that for 10 years.

That is until somebody said, "Hey, have you seen this thing with you on this meme?" I was like, "What meme? What's a *meme*? I don't even know what a meme *is*." "It's you, saying, "It's Over 9,000!" Somebody put it on the Internet." "Really? What?!"

It was a joke, and so ridiculous. I was embarrassed about it at first. I thought, 'Oh god, that line's *terrible*! Why would you pick my worst-performed line?' Because I was forced to do it that way because of the lip flaps—why would they choose *that* to be a meme that people talk about? It's because there was something bizarre and funny about it, and that's what the Internet has become: the place of the bizarre and funny. And it took off.

Now I have to scream it multiple times at conventions. So I say, "You only

---

1   Karl Willems was the director of the *Dragon Ball Z* Ocean dub.

get a few at this convention. Too many and I'll lose my voice. So come early!"

Q: It's such a big thing that I've written a book about it. And Ronda Rousey recently wore an "It's Over 9,000!" shirt at her Wrestlemania event. How does the meme's success make you feel?

I try not to look at these things as if they have anything to do with me. Even though it was my voice behind those sounds, there is an animator's animation that makes the lips flap that way, a director who said, "No Brian, we need you to hold the 'nine thousand,'" and a *YouTube* user who put it together in a crazy meme: if he had not done that, it would have disappeared. So it's not like what I did made it appear. It's a combination of a number of things. Which is sometimes how something takes off on the Internet. It's a combination of forces that came together: my voice, in a bizarre read, that somebody heard and thought, 'That's so weird how that guy read that,' and then put it together in a clip that said it over and over again. Everybody forwarded it around because it was so weird. Then over time it loses the weird, and becomes not weird, but cool, and super hot, and super awesome. When something's "Over Nine Thousaaaaaaand!" it's awesome now. It's a chant for something like, "Let's do thiiiiiiiis!" You can hold it. That's what it is now, and it's still changing. Who knows what it will mean 20 years from now.

But it puts a smile on my face when I think about it. I think it puts a smile on a lot of other people's faces. And it put a smile on Ronda Rousey's face when she decided to wear that shirt. She probably had any number of options, including a shirt with advertising on it to make her some money. But she chose to wear a shirt with Vegeta from *Dragon Ball Z*. I hope she grew up watching Vegeta and hearing me scream that. That would make me happy.

Q: She's a huge Vegeta fan and loves the show.

Awesome. I hope I meet her someday. I'm thinking it would be fun if on October 17, 2016, 10 years from the day the meme was launched on the Internet, maybe Chris Sabat and I will have a scream off at a convention. Maybe we'll get Ronda to show up too, who knows, haha. We'll do a '10 Year Anniversary of "Over 9,000!"'

Q: How do you feel about Chris Sabat having to do the line because you did it?

Oh, I know. Haha. I feel really bad for him about that. I feel terrible that he has to do that line and then constantly say, "Well, it wasn't me who did that version."

But then when I go to a convention in the US and someone says, "Oh, do Vegeta's voice!" and I do my version of Vegeta, they say, "Oh, that's not quite what I remember." And I have to 'Chris Sabatize' my voice: [deepens his voice] "You're used to the Vegeta that's from *here* [lower in the throat], sounds much more *noble* as opposed to mine." They say, "Yeah, that's him!" I'm like, "Yeah... that's Chris Sabat."

So he gets to put up with my crazy fan club and I get to put up with his. I'm sure we're both pretty cool with it.

Brian Drummond,

2015

ABOUT THE AUTHOR

DEREK PADULA IS the author of *The Dao of Dragon Ball* website and book series; the first to reveal the history, philosophy, and culture of the world's #1 anime and manga.

Derek first saw the *Dragon Ball* anime in 1997. His love for the series inspired him to start martial arts training in Shàolín *gōngfu*, *tàijí-quán*, *qìgōng*, *karate*, and *fǎlún dàfǎ* meditation. He earned his B.A. in East Asian Studies and a minor in Chinese from Western Michigan University. He studied abroad in Běijīng, China and trained with the Buddhist Shàolín monks and a Dàoist *tàijí* sword master. After returning home, he became an authority on *Dragon Ball*.

Next Steps …

Buy *The Dao of Dragon Ball* Books

The Dao of Dragon Ball books are filled with insights, history, and fascinating connections to ancient martial arts principles and spiritual beliefs. They also reveal the full history of the series, its impact on the world, and the inner meaning of the #1 action anime of all time.

Books:

Dragon Ball Culture Volumes 1 to 7

Dragon Soul: 30 Years of Dragon Ball Fandom

Dragon Ball Cultura Volumen 1 (Spanish Edition)

Dragon Ball Z "It's Over 9,000!" Cosmovisiones en colisión (Spanish Edition)

Read *The Dao of Dragon Ball* Website

The Dao of Dragon Ball website is written to share insights on *Dragon Ball* and have discussions with fans. Join in!

Have the latest blog posts delivered directly to you for free via e-mail.

Write to the Author

If you have questions or comments about this book, then write Derek at:

https://thedaoofdragonball.com/

INDEX

REFERENCES

DRAGON BALL INFO

Dragon Ball Kai episode list:
http://en.wikipedia.org/wiki/List_of_Dragon_Ball_Kai_episodes

Kanzentai.com Battle Power Guide:
http://www.kanzentai.com/bp.php?id=manga

Snake Way:
http://dragonball.wikia.com/wiki/Snake_Way

MULTIMEDIA

Dragon Box Volume 1 DVD Box Set. Dragon Ball Z DVD Box Volume 1.
TOEI Animation Co., Ltd., FUNimation Productions Ltd.

SOCIAL NEWS

Google Insights on "over 9,000":
http://www.google.com/insights/search/#q=%2C%22over%20
9000%22%2C&cmpt=q

Google Trends for "over 9,000":
http://www.google.com/trends?q=over+9000

Interview with Kajetokun:
http://www.japanator.com/elephant/post.phtml?pk=7824

Know Your Meme's "It's Over 9,000!" page:
http://knowyourmeme.com/memes/its-over-9000

Oprah Winfrey joke:
http://www.newsgroper.com/samuel-l-jackson/2008/09/20/9000-penises-oprah-winfrey-child-porn-and-my-got-damn-mojito

Freddie Wong's Video Game High School on Kickstarter:
http://www.kickstarter.com/projects/freddiew/video-game-high-school

Dragon Ball is #1 in Oricon Study:
http://www.crunchyroll.com/anime-news/2012/08/07-1/dragon-ball-takes-the-gold-in-oricon-ranking-of-top-10-world-class-anime

Videos

The original "It's Over 9,000!" video:
http://www.youtube.com/watch?v=TBtpyeLxVkI

The original "It's Over 8,000!" clip:
http://www.youtube.com/watch?v=z9NMy6hVJpo

"It's Over 9,000!" Dub comparison:
http://www.youtube.com/watch?v=CLEzZGosqe8

"It's Over 9,000!" in Dragon Ball Z:
Burst Limit: http://www.youtube.com/watch?v=bRthvdLlLnY

Freddie Wong's Live-Action "It's Over 9,000!":
http://www.youtube.com/watch?v=LHqEwIadhO8

Michael Jordan says, "I've missed more than 9,000 shots in my career":
http://www.youtube.com/watch?v=c32KHyvLnxM

Marshall Mcluhan Interview:
http://www.youtube.com/watch?v=ImaH51F4HBw

Marshall Mcluhan Canadian Heritage Commercial:
http://www.youtube.com/watch?v=RtycdRBAbXk

Jalen's Super Saiyans are Real:
http://www.youtube.com/watch?v=fYxCrugJj_o

Printed in Great Britain
by Amazon

77183804R00061